MINE'S A DOUBLE

The Twins Book

Sue Mortimer

Sue Mortimer

First published in 2011 by

Life Publications
Merthyr Tydfil, South Wales, UK
davidholdaway1@aol.com

To order further copies e-mail
thetwinsbook@aol.co.uk

ISBN 978-190792-905-2

Contents

1 **Introduction**   7
    Much ado about twins?
    A twin is for life

2 **In the Beginning**   13
    Twin pregnancies
        Twins are what you get ...
        A tale of two babies
        An operatic encore
        Have you taken your pill, darling?
        Easy for some ....
        ....Tricky for others

3 **Help for the Stork**   27
    Conception by IVF
        Great expectations. The IVF era
        Sixth time lucky
        Two sisters
        Repeat order
        Getting pregnant on holiday
        Upgraded to twins

4 **Special Delivery**   39
    Twin births
        Twins squared
        In for the long haul
        She scored twice ...
        Taken by surprise
        Two's too many
        Easy peasy

5 **An Extra Mouth to Feed**   53
    Living with baby and toddler twins
        What parents say
        Leave it to Auntie
        Feeding-time talk

5   **(Continued)**
     Stung by curiosity
     In the limelight
     Twin trauma
     Nicer than the nick

6   **One Is One, but Two Are Trouble**   67
    From toddlers to teenagers
     Can we play quietly, please?
     Party poopers
     Highway to hell?
     On location
     Sir! Sir! The bell's gone
     A pair? Or only brother and sister?
     'It's cool to be a twin!'

7   **And Three's a Crowd**   83
    Triplets and more
     Three of a kind
     Increasing the odds
     Touch and go
     Peas in a pod
     Three cheers for playtime!
     Oh my quad!
     Hit for six?

8   **The Quad Father**   95
    Living with four
     From here to maternity
     Publicity and practicality
     The limits of independence
     Going potty!
     Child's play

9   **You Only Live Twice**   105
    Twins in the adult world
     Double Firsts
     Twins, or just born at the same time?
     Dead ringers
     Labour's double whammy
     Life in triplicate

10   Separate Lives   121
   Twins separated by circumstances
      The wall in our heads
      Twins reunited
      Separated by murder

11   Life in Tandem   135
   Twins in the family
      As they say ....
      Do they run in the family?
      Twintuition?
      It's grand to be a grandad
      Well-known twins
      Unknown twins

12   Seeing Double   149
   At the twins' convention
      Twins galore
      Second impressions
      Private investigations
      Redoubled efforts

13   A Risky Business   159
   When things go wrong with twin births
      Physician, heal thyself
      When your twin can threaten your life
      The worst of starts
      Living with disability
      Pluck from the memory a rooted sorrow
      Orphaned at birth

14   Double Figures   173
   Twins. The facts and the statistics
      What and Why and When ...

15   Spitting Images?   185
   The facts about 'doubles'
      One face, one voice, one habit ...

Much ado about twins?

There are about one and a quarter million twins living in Britain today, and some twenty-five thousand new ones are born each year, almost twice as many as thirty years ago. Twins attract attention, whether they be month-old babies or look-alike eighty-year-old men. So many people *are* twins, *have* twins, are grandparents or relatives of twins, have friends who have twins, know twins from school or socially, or are simply interested in the strange phenomenon of life in duplicate.

What is it like to *have* twins? What is it like to *be* a twin? What are the risks in having twins? How do twins differ from other children? Do adult twins still feel 'different'? How does a twin cope with losing the 'other half'? Are identical twins really identical, and what does that mean in practice? And what if there are more than two – triplets or more?

So many questions. Every twin, every parent of twins, even more so every prospective parent of twins, must wonder about these things. At best, books can only provide a partial answer, but most of the available books do not even do that. In seeking generalisation, they overlook the fact that in the end experiences are individual. As with other aspects of life, there are no prescriptive manuals.

This book is neither a medical treatise nor a parenting guide. Instead its basis is that, although they won't be the same, other people's experiences are the best source of information about life as or with twins. No conclusions are drawn. No advice is offered. Instead, the real stories of real people, as related to the author in personal interviews, are simply and briefly set down. The reader can take as much, or as little, from each as he or she finds relevant and interesting. If there is a 'message', it is that most twins, and most parents of twins, wouldn't have it any other way.

The last two chapters are different. Here the facts and the relevant figures about twins, identical twins, and other multiples are set out as background to the actual experiences reported in the main part of the book. Some may find these chapters superfluous. Others may want to read them first, in order to put the individual experiences into their wider context. Like the book as a whole, this is a matter of choice. The chapters progress logically from conception to adult life, but each individual story is complete in itself. Read the book how you will!

The final chapters are also different in that they use case studies drawn from the wider media in order to illustrate the more unusual situations which may arise. In the remainder of the book the author sets down in good faith the experiences reported to her face to face by the individuals concerned. In order to preserve the privacy of these contributors first names only have been used, and in many cases even these, but not the other facts, have been changed.

To declare an interest, the author has her own twins, seven years of age at the time of writing, and they also appear in these pages, but not necessarily under their own names.

Acknowledgements

The author gratefully acknowledges the help given by the following during the preparation of this book.

Dr Sujoy Banerjee, Consultant Neonatologist
Jane Denton, CBE, FRCN, RGN, RM, Director, The Multiple Births Foundation
Dr Rhian Fuge, Consultant Haematologist
Hartmut Hartleb, President of Germany's ABC Club for triplets and higher-order multiples
Dr Elizabeth MacGowan, General Practitioner
Professor David Skibinski, Professor of Evolutionary Biology, Swansea University

Organisations and websites

The Multiple Births Foundation (www.multiplebirths.org.uk)
TAMBA, The Twins and Multiple Births Association (www.tamba.org.uk)
The Lone Twin Network (www.lonetwinnetwork.org.uk)
Germany's ABC Club - see above; website also in English (www.abc-club.de)

A twin is for life

At the age of eighty identical twins Alf and Joe are still living together

"Ere you! You've 'ad yer grub', shouted the mess sergeant. 'No I haven't', replied Private Joe hungrily. 'That must have been my twin brother.' 'A likely tale', snorted the sergeant. 'Fetch him then.' So poor Joe had to hunt out Alf from their billet before he could eat. It could have been worse. As babies they were so alike that once their mother fed Alf twice while Joe got nothing.

Just a couple of the odd incidents that happen to twins in the course of a long life. Eighty years to be precise. Or eighty not out, to be even more accurate, because Alf and Joe are still together, living by the sea in Swansea with Alf's wife Jean. Joe doesn't drive any more, so he shares Alf's car, just as they shared a car when they could first afford to buy one half a century ago. Happily they didn't fight over it then like they did over the very first car, 'the only real fight we've ever had', Alf remembers. Granny had bought Joe a pedal car with shiny wheels and electric lights – quite something in the 1930s – while Alf got a rocking horse. Poor Granny hadn't read lesson one in the book on twins psychology, but she picked up the general idea after Alf had dragged Joe off the car by his hair, denting the bonnet in the process as the punch-up moved outside. The horse went back to the shop next day and Alf got wheels of his own, not quite as flash maybe, but boyish honour was satisfied.

Born in Tredegar, South Wales, in 1928, the boys, as they are still known today, were nearly separated from the outset. At nine pounds apiece they gave Mum a hard time even before the birth, when she would only go out after dark so that no one would notice the size of her belly. The delivery, in Granny's front room and with Auntie, Tredegar's only midwife, in attendance, came close to tragedy. Mum pulled through but Dad wasn't taking any more chances, so the twins have no other siblings. Meanwhile a well-intentioned uncle offered to take one of the boys to ease the burden on the tired mother, but fortunately he was politely but firmly refused.

The next time separation threatened was in 1947, when Alf was called up for National Service. By then the twins were working in separate engineering companies, but as Joe's employer was busy with essential post-war reconstruction he was exempt from the call-up. So he volunteered. 'What's two years out of a lifetime?', he said. Joe must have been a fast talker, as he not only convinced an army board to let him join up despite his essential occupation, but he also persuaded the military to keep the brothers together for the next two years, most of it in Egypt.

Back in Scunthorpe, where the family had moved during the Depression when the boys were five, the tall, dark and handsome brothers turned a few heads. 'The handsomest men in Scunthorpe', Jean called them, 'but I could always tell the difference, and anyway they were different personalities.' Others were not so perceptive. One Saturday Alf was standing in the street waiting for Jean to finish shopping when a total stranger came up and engaged him in a long conversation. Alf was baffled until the stranger went on his way with the parting words: 'See you in work on Monday, Joe.'

The twins are used to causing confusion separately and to attracting attention together, something which began when they were babies and which still happens to them as elderly men. 'Often if we go somewhere together we will arrive and leave separately to avoid the whispers of "Look! They're twins"', says Joe. But they had to laugh on one occasion, when they all went to church with Alf's young son Peter, causing a little girl to break the silence before the service with a loud stage whisper: 'Look Mummy. Peter's got two daddies.'

The bond between the brothers has always been strong, comparable to that between their parents, they say. As was then usual, they both lived with their parents as young adults, until Alf married at the age of 32. Joe stayed at home, eventually looking after their ageing father when their mother died, but Alf and his family were just around the corner. Once Joe fell and broke his arm at work, and Alf recalls his own experience. 'I didn't feel a pain or anything', he says, 'but around the time of the accident I had a strange feeling of unease, which I didn't understand until I got home and found out what had happened to Joe.'

The perfect gift

for a twin, the parents or grandparents of twins, or those expecting twins

A copy of this book!

Enquiries and orders by e-mail to

thetwinsbook@aol.co.uk

Twins are what you get ...
when you go to bed with hiccups
(Attributed to Ken Dodd, comedian)

Baby number two turned out to be numbers two and three

Two little faces could be seen slumbering in the all-terrain buggy. Designed for off-pavement country paths, its smooth suspension was not strictly necessary in London's urban jungle. Yet it served its purpose as five-month-old Toby and Martha dozed in the fresh autumn air.

Rachel and Steve had been delighted when the pregnancy test was positive, eagerly anticipating a sibling for two-year-old Ben. Even when the sonographer at the twelve-week scan enquired whether there were twins in the family, Rachel assumed this was just friendly chat. Then there was an awkward silence. 'Are you telling us there are two babies?' Rachel could not conceal the anxiety in her voice as the idea started to sink in. Looking back, she realised that this pregnancy had been different from her first. She had felt more tired and lethargic, and she was definitely larger, but she had attributed this to stomach muscles slackened during the first pregnancy, and not to twins.

Still reeling from the shock, the couple next faced the nuchal scan, a test for chromosomal abnormality associated with Down's syndrome. The risk is calculated using the mother's age, her hormone levels, the amount of fluid behind the baby's neck, and the length of the baby. The measurements of each twin were carefully recorded, and the other figures were factored in, but the results were worryingly high. Fortunately when the sonographer checked her calculations an error was discovered, and the risk was in fact extremely low. Both babies should be healthy. Nevertheless it had been a traumatic morning for Rachel and Steve, as the happily awaited single baby had first become twins, and had then presented the possibility of Down's syndrome. Calming down over a cup of coffee, they called their parents to share their news.

Two days after the scan Rachel had a bleed. Now she was frightened by the prospect of losing the twins, who had already become a part of her life. Although the incident passed over safely it left her anxious, as it brought home to her that a twin pregnancy

14

has higher risks, both for the mother and for the babies. While friends laughingly congratulated her on 'double trouble', her mind was focused on the potential dangers. The babies might be premature, they might have health problems arising from a low birth weight, or they might not even survive. Happily in most cases such fears prove unfounded, and so it was with Rachel. At week 38 she gave birth naturally to two healthy babies, Toby, weighing 3.3 kg (7 lb 3 oz), followed thirteen minutes later by Martha, at 3.5 kg (7 lb 11 oz).

A tale of two babies

Samantha knew from an early stage that she was expecting twins ....

.... but she was left reeling after the 29-week scan, when the doctor confirmed that the babies were on course for birth weights of up to 3.6 kg (8 lb) apiece. The prospect of carrying two such brutes to full term was daunting, and the thought of pushing them out was positively terrifying. A friend jokingly suggested that she took up smoking; perhaps that might reduce the babies' final size! As a militant non-smoker Samantha could at least see the funny side.

From the outset the pregnancy had been problematic. Samantha had just recovered from a previous miscarriage, and she had a long-standing medical condition which might compromise both the pregnancy and her own health. At eight weeks all seemed lost. During an important meeting she felt a sudden rush of blood, and she had to dash out. To her great relief a scan some days later showed two embryos pulsating with life. Not only was she pregnant, but it was twins! Moreover they survived another bleed a couple of weeks later. Samantha was determined to hang on to those precious lives.

The pregnancy required close medical supervision, but the twelve-week scan was a revelation, as the babies, like tiny marionettes, alternated between jogging and kicking each other in the head. Samantha wondered how they – or she – would survive this ordeal. By week sixteen one had been identified as a boy, and a second boy was confirmed soon after. Male obstinacy was soon in evidence. At a twenty-week scan to check the babies' development, it took three separate attempts for all the measurements to be completed, as the twins refused to play ball. Not even Samantha doing star jumps in the corridor could coax them both to move into position for the scan.

Like many expectant mothers, Samantha was susceptible to sickness, but the high hormone levels with twins often makes it worse. Fighting the nausea became part of the daily routine. Wake up, eat, throw up at home, and again on the way to work. After a brief spell at her desk, hoping to shake off this permanent 'hangover', she would sneak out to satisfy her craving for a greasy breakfast. Soon the rush to the toilet would start up again, and so it went on all day. Morning sickness was clearly a misnomer. Thoughts of overtime were banished, and she left the office punctually each afternoon, hoping to make it home before being sick again. Her colleagues even suspected that Samantha was struggling with alcohol. Nothing was further from the truth.

Each day Samantha's stomach grew, and even maternity clothes felt tight. 'You can tell it's twins!', a friend exclaimed, noting that the double bump at week 27 was bigger than hers had been at week 40. People frequently commented that the baby must be overdue, even though the twins had two months to go. A shop assistant, the soul of tact, observed loudly: 'I've never seen such a big belly in my life!' Sleeping became increasingly difficult, and lying on her back was out of the question with the weight of the double pregnancy pressing down on her. She could only doze fitfully, sitting upright, before the babies stirred at dawn. 'It felt like an octopus practising for the World Cup!'

Aches and pains appeared as the babies jostled Samantha's organs, pushing them aside as they grew. Even her lungs were squeezed, making the slightest exertion hard work. By week 29 climbing a flight of stairs left her breathless. Then she developed a painful condition in the pelvic region, as ligaments became overstretched in response to pregnancy hormones. This symphysis pubis dysfunction – or 'syphilis', as her mother announced to her friends! – restricted Samantha's movements, and the doctor advised against walks of longer than ten minutes. Nor would her bump fit comfortably behind the steering wheel, so she was increasingly reliant on lifts.

By week 31 her blood pressure was raised, and there were traces of protein in her urine. This could indicate a more serious condition, pre-eclampsia, and the doctors were concerned. Expectant mothers of twins are more likely to suffer from this problem than those carrying a single baby. Yet Samantha felt fine, apart from the discomfort of her twin burden. 'I *can't* get any bigger', she found herself saying, as if responding to a message from her body. And she was right. She went into labour that day, and her two boys were born, healthy even though nearly two months early, and each weighing 1.8 kg (4 lb).

An operatic encore

From prima donna to the mother of twins, and back again

As a promising teenager Sinéad moved with her family from Ireland to the United States, where she was soon singing in New York productions of *Grease* and *Cabaret*. Then a musical director suggested that her voice was ideally suited to opera. She took the advice, and despite having only a basic knowledge of classical music she was accepted as a pupil at the highly acclaimed Juilliard School in New York, going on later to take a Master's degree at the Curtis Institute in Philadelphia. Her debut was at the Opéra in Paris, and just two years later the gifted soprano moved to Germany, to take up a prestigious post at one of Berlin's three opera houses, the Komische Oper.

When she got married, Sinéad hoped that babies could be fitted around her singing schedule, although husband David was sceptical, as 'the best-laid schemes o' mice an' men gang aft a-gley'. Nevertheless, she thought, having a summer baby would fit in with the opera season, and she would be able to sing until shortly before the birth. Soon she suspected that she was pregnant, but she was startled by the very positive result of an early test. 'It almost jumped out of my hand!'

The first ultrasound scan showed a single baby, and Sinéad continued with her schedule, singing five performances in a demanding operatic role, but she was overcome by nausea at nine weeks. Unable to keep food down, she was admitted to hospital, where she had another scan to check on the baby's health. This time there were two babies on the screen, and David and Sinéad couldn't contain their laughter and delight.

On the down side, Sinéad had to give up her plan to have the confinement at a midwife-run birthing centre, as only a hospital would accept a potentially high-risk twin delivery. David was relieved, preferring the security of doctors and technical support. Sinéad also had to stay in hospital for ten days, receiving fluids intravenously, before she was discharged, and it was not until the severe sickness abated, after the fourth month, that she started to enjoy being pregnant. Nor could she continue to appear on stage, as her twin pregnancy was considered too high a risk by the opera house's insurers, and she had to stop performing completely after a recital in month five, as she could no longer hit her top notes. The twins were taking up too much space in her body, and her breathing was becoming increasingly difficult.

A natural delivery was essential if Sinéad were to resume work quickly, as a Caesarean section would damage muscles vital for singing, requiring a prolonged recovery period. By the end of week 37 the doctors advised her that labour should be induced, as otherwise the babies might grow too big for a normal birth. Yet despite the best medical efforts the twins were determined to wait in the wings, and not to appear centre stage just yet. Sinéad was equally determined, holding out for a natural delivery even though the prospect of a Caesarean to bring the exhausting process to an end seemed enticing. 'That wasn't a good enough reason for me.' At the end of week 38 she was induced again, and this time it worked. Sinéad pushed Isabelle out, followed two minutes later by Emilie, each weighing in at 2.7 kg (6 lb), an experience which she describes as 'just incredible'.

The following day Sinéad started to hum familiar tunes, and each day she practised singing in the odd few free moments her twins left her. The pregnancy had stretched her muscles out of shape, and after the long break from singing it was a struggle to regain her full powers. Yet she persisted, and within nine months her voice returned to its former glory. Meanwhile she chose her work carefully. Her first concert, just twelve weeks after the birth, was a gentle re-introduction, requiring only seven minutes of actual singing. Gradually she eased herself into more demanding roles. The First Lady in *The Magic Flute* was perfectly suited to her voice, and soon she graduated to Micaëla in *Carmen*, a role with twenty minutes of singing. After several months she was able to sing the leading part in Janáček's *Jenufa*, a role she had performed before her pregnancy. The soprano gave a bravura performance, to match her double achievement as a mother.

Have you taken your pill, darling?

A double shock was in store for Susanne, who became pregnant with twins while taking the contraceptive pill

Returning from a skiing holiday, she felt unusually lethargic, her legs ached, and her feet were swollen. She had no plans for more children, as her energies were channelled into her job and looking after her eight-year-old daughter. Yet despite being on the pill she began to wonder if she might be pregnant, and a missed period prompted her to take a test. Her suspicions were confirmed. 'The pregnancy was a welcome surprise!'

Susanne had to wait a fortnight until her first scan, and memories of an earlier miscarriage returned to haunt her. 'I wanted to stop myself from becoming emotionally attached to this pregnancy.' Her concerns were heightened by a bleed just before her visit to the clinic, but her anxiety quickly vanished as the screen showed the baby's heart beating with reassuring regularity. Then a closer look showed a second sac, tucked almost out of sight behind the first one. The doctor quickly dismissed Susanne's thought that this might be a second baby, explaining that in early pregnancy it was not uncommon to see an empty sac, and that this would soon disappear.

A fortnight later, despite severe nausea, she managed to drag herself to the clinic again. This time the scan was quite clear, and Susanne was amazed to see two pulsating heartbeats. The doctor shared her surprise. 'I hadn't expected that at all, but there really are two babies!' Susanne had conceived twins while taking the contraceptive pill! Thoughts flashed through her mind. What about her job? Would the flat and the car be big enough? A telephone call to the delighted father set her mind at rest. Everything would sort itself out somehow. Coping with everyday life with two little ones would be challenging, but her husband's unhesitating support boosted her confidence.

The pregnancy with Alicia had gone to plan. The sickness had abated after the first twelve weeks, and the birth had been on the due date and without complications. This time the pregnancy was classed as high-risk, involving fortnightly check-ups. Susanne was already feeling big by week 25, when she went for a routine visit to the clinic before a family holiday. During the examination the doctor became suddenly anxious, and then explained that the amniotic sac of the lower-lying twin was visible through the partially opened cervix. Travel plans were abandoned, and instead an ambulance was called to take her to hospital.

Preserving the pregnancy was now Susanne's sole priority, and she was under strict instructions to lie as still as possible for the remaining time. After five weeks she was allowed to get up once a day for the toilet, and once a week for a shower. She began to wonder whether so much inactivity would leave her with the strength for childbirth, yet she counted each day as a bonus, increasing the twins' potential for survival and reducing their risk of longer-term health problems. The wait seemed an eternity, until at week 32 contractions began, and Sebastian and Delf were born. Susanne was now mother to small but healthy twin boys, each weighing 1.8 kg (3 lb 14 oz). Her strength soon returned, but it would be a while before she went skiing again.

Easy for some ....

While some women struggle to conceive, others become pregnant with no apparent effort, and certain ethnic groups are particularly prone to twins

Doris is an expert on twins. She grew up surrounded by them in her native Nigeria, and then she had two sets of her own with her British husband. Her first pair were girls, and the second a boy and a girl. Her sister has young twins, and there are more on both their mother's and their father's sides of the family.

Nigeria tops the international league table for naturally conceived non-identical twins. These occur at a rate estimated to be nearly five times higher among the Yoruba ethnic group than in the rest of the world. The reasons are not fully established, although there is probably a hereditary genetic link, much as fraternal twins crop up repeatedly in some families elsewhere. Many locals prefer the traditional idea that twins are a special blessing bestowed by God, while some believe that there is a link between eating large amounts of yam (sweet potato) and the occurrence of twins, as the local variety contains oestrogen-like chemicals which may encourage a woman's body to release multiple eggs. A friend in Nigeria quipped: 'Doris, with two sets of twins you should cut out the yam!' Scientists, though, remain sceptical about the influence of diet on female fertility.

According to Yoruba tradition, twins have separate bodies but share one soul. *Taiyewo* ('the first to sample the world') is the name given to the one who emerges first. Based on what he or she sees, the cries of this baby determine whether the second sibling, *Kehinde* ('the last to arrive'), is born alive or not. The second-born twin is regarded as the true elder, as the *Taiyewo* came out first in deference to the unborn sibling's authority. Doris was at school with Yoruba twins, where the *Kehinde* was in her class while the *Taiyewo* sister was in a different group.

Newborn twins are seen as a special gift, and the community celebrates their arrival. The parents provide a meal of black-eyed beans, or *ewa*, also known as twin food, in exchange for the presents they receive. The mother sings and dances while carrying her babies in a 'wrapper', one on her back and one on her belly.

In her resonant voice Doris sings a traditional Yoruba song for twins, like a soothing lullaby, which she translates into English:

> If I have twins, I am going to carry them,
> If I give birth to twins, I am going to carry them,
> I am not scared, I am not afraid,
> If I have twins, I will carry them.

Even though twins are a common sight in Nigeria, Doris and her family caused a stir during a visit to the country's capital, Lagos. Accompanied by both sets of twins and her Caucasian husband, Doris was surprised by the stares of passers-by. Finally she understood, as she overheard a loud whisper: 'I never knew white people had twins!'

....Tricky for others

Tracey found that she was expecting two babies while living in Japan, a country with one of the world's lowest rates of naturally conceived non-identical twins

'What is this?' Tracey knew enough Japanese to understand the doctor's words, but it was his shocked tone that unsettled her. He switched to broken English. 'You have two babies!' Moments later the examination room was crowded with doctors and nurses keen to glimpse this rare sight.

Derek's job had taken them from their native New Zealand to the Japanese city of Fukuoka, where they had decided to start their family. Following two miscarriages Tracey was becoming despondent. 'That's when I began to feel odd and noticed I was going to the toilet more than usual. So I decided to try a pregnancy test.' It should have been too early, as her period wasn't due for another five days. Yet the clear blue line was unmistakeable.

She headed straight for the maternity clinic, where the doctor agreed that the test appeared positive. She should, he said, come back six days later, by which time her period would be overdue and he could test her. It seemed a long wait, during which Tracey fretted about losing the baby and sought reassurance from numerous test kits, but finally the doctor confirmed the pregnancy.

The first scan was scheduled for her fourth week. In the waiting room Tracey stared open-mouthed at the attention lavished on the pregnant women. Against a background of soft classical music a fountain splashed gently into a pond, as each patient was greeted and swaddled in a blanket. The mothers-to-be were then offered a hand or a foot massage. It was more like a beauty clinic than a hospital.

Derek had to wait outside as Tracey was called in to the scanning room. After undressing she sat in the examination chair, where the nurse covered her up – presumably to preserve her modesty – before allowing her husband in. Derek stood by her head, and they had their own monitor during the scan. She was discreetly separated from the medical team by a flimsy net curtain, which masked her face. Before she knew it, the doctor had swung the chair around, and her legs flopped apart ready for the internal examination.

Feeling naked, Tracey had not anticipated the amount of interest she would generate. The small room was now full of medical staff craning for a good view. She alternated between shock at the news of twins and embarrassment at her exposed position. There were indeed two sacs, although it was too early to see heartbeats. Twins had crossed her mind, but Derek had dismissed the idea on the way to the clinic that morning. But one of her miscarriages *had* been suspected twins, and there *were* several sets in her family. Now they faced the startling reality of two babies on the way.

Tracey soon realised just how special twins are in Japan. Not once did she see a twin pushchair in the streets. 'I don't think it would have been easy to buy a double buggy there.' The high level of interest in the twins at the initial scan was maintained at subsequent appointments, and she noticed that extra staff were always present to learn about a twin pregnancy. 'All the pregnant women were treated wonderfully, but the doctors followed our case particularly closely', she recalls.

At week 26 they flew back to New Zealand to await the babies' arrival, but four weeks later Tracey was admitted to hospital with raised blood pressure and traces of protein in her urine, the first symptoms of pre-eclampsia. By week 33 the doctors decided that they had to get the babies out. Tracey had been drifting in and out of consciousness, but she managed to stay awake for the Caesarean section. As the surgical team positioned a screen over her stomach to spare her the gore, she thought back to the net curtain in Japan all those months ago. Then she caught sight of her two little girls emerging, premature but healthy.

Great expectations. The IVF era

The world's first test-tube baby, Louise Brown, was born in Britain in 1978

In 2009 some 15,000 IVF babies were born in Britain alone, and many, many times more world-wide. Some facts and figures are given in Chapter 14 of this book, but as with natural pregnancies each case is not merely a number but an individual story. Mrs Brown, Louise's mother, is still counting her blessings. 'I'm just so grateful that I'm a mum at all, because without IVF I never would have been.' Her daughter was even more fortunate. Her own child – Mrs Brown's grandchild – was naturally conceived.

Some of the cost of infertility treatment is now commonly met by public funding, at least in Britain, but most of the couples seeking help end up footing at least part of the bill, and if many tries are required the cost can be high. One expectant mother commented that they might as well splash out on two new Moses baskets for their prospective twins. 'After all, these babies have cost us £13,000.' Yet compared to the efforts of Neil and Monique that was just loose change. In their pursuit of a baby, which took 25 years, they spent £100,000 before finally hitting the jackpot. In 2009, after travelling to a clinic in Spain, their twin boys Benjamin and Walker were born, giving a happy end to this tale.

IVF can also help in the most extreme cases of infertility, sometimes even involving a surrogate mother carrying an implanted embryo through to birth on behalf of the biological parents. After treatment for cancer, Anne Maria could no longer conceive naturally, but she did have a supply of fertilised embryos, which had been prepared in advance and frozen for later use. Sadly, a series of attempts failed, leading her to have one last-ditch try at becoming a mother. Doctors in New York agreed to implant two of the remaining four embryos into her, and two into her sister, who had volunteered to help by acting as a surrogate. Much to everyone's surprise, two sets of twins were born, ten days apart, together making up perhaps the most unusual set of quads so far known. Celebrities such as Sarah Jessica Parker and Ricky Martin are also among those who have become parents to twins using a surrogate mother.

New techniques, however, can also bring new problems, or give a new twist to old problems. Tragic stories occasionally come to light of babies swapped on the maternity ward, and growing up apart from their biological families (see Chapter 15). With IVF such blunders, whilst rare, are possible in the laboratory. In 2002 one black and one white 'twin' were born to a white couple after a mix-up at a New York IVF clinic. However emotional links can be as powerful as biological ones, and the 'stowaway' baby was only returned to the black couple who were its natural parents after a legal battle for custody.

Likewise, while IVF can be a boon for childless women past their fertility peak and approaching the dreaded 40th birthday, there are always some who will push the limits to the extremes. One Spanish woman became the mother of twin boys at the age of 66, after apparently lying about her age in order to obtain treatment in the USA, using donor eggs and sperm. Tragically, the children are now orphans, as she died of cancer in 2009, when they were two. Nor are such excesses confined to the western world. In 2008 a 70-year-old grandmother gave birth to twins in India, after her 77-year-old husband sold his buffalos, mortgaged his land and spent his life savings to fund IVF, hoping to produce a male heir.

Among the most extraordinary examples of the pursuit of the possible is the case of a woman who stole the world's headlines when she delivered octuplets in California in 2009. Still more startling, she already had six young children, including one set of twins, and all fourteen children were conceived using IVF. This spectacular multiple birth sparked much debate, and has drawn attention to the way in which technological breakthroughs bring the need for regulation in their train. In the UK transfers of more than two embryos in a single cycle (other than in special cases) are actively discouraged by the relevant authority.

Sixth time lucky

Like Robert Bruce's spider, Mary and Roger had to try, try and try again

The phone rang at Mary's desk. She hesitated before answering. 'This is the infertility clinic. Can you talk?', the nurse asked. 'No, but you go ahead', she replied. Mary's heart started to race, and she hoped that her colleagues were out of earshot. 'We've got the blood test results. They are very positive. It may even be twins.' Dazed, she left the office for a short walk in the fresh air.

This was her sixth IVF treatment, three years on from the start. The first pregnancy test at the hospital had been negative, although she 'felt' pregnant and a home-test kit had shown encouraging signs of the tell-tale blue line developing. A repeat visit a week later was equally disappointing. 'You might have been pregnant, but we will never know.' She had then requested the blood test.

Like many couples, their only hope of becoming parents had been IVF. Attempts to reverse Roger's vasectomy had failed, so some of his sperm had been extracted and frozen. Single sperm were to be injected into each egg harvested from Mary, using the ICSI technique. First heavy doses of drugs were needed to suppress her natural menstrual cycle, and then she had to inject herself daily to encourage the ovarian follicles to produce eggs. 'It felt like the menopause each time, followed by a bloated belly as the follicles grew. It was hormonal hell.' Their early IVF attempts had been promising, with two high-quality embryos implanted each time, but then nothing. Just disappointment as Mary's period heralded failure yet again. Life was on hold, fitted in briefly between treatment cycles and revolving around planning and timetables. They confided in no one about the IVF. Time enough to tell the world if successful; better to shoulder the disappointment alone if not. Their medical notes became ever thicker, their bank account slimmer, and their hearts heavier.

On their first visit to the clinic they had been overwhelmed by the myriad photos of babies smiling down from the walls, but their initial expectations of a ready-made take-away family were soon dashed.

Nothing was straightforward. On the first treatment a cyst had to be lanced, slowing down progress. The fourth was abandoned just before the egg collection. Mary's abdominal pain had been diagnosed as ovarian hyperstimulation, a potentially serious side effect of IVF. They seemed to have turned the corner at the fifth cycle, after being invited to take part in trials of blastocyst transfers. This meant that the fertilised embryos were left to grow in the laboratory for longer than the two to three days of standard IVF. Two blastocysts were implanted five days after fertilisation, but the doctors were not happy with the faint blue line on the pregnancy test and a negative scan two weeks later. They suspected an ectopic pregnancy, a condition whereby a fertilised egg implants outside the womb, and which could have dangerous consequences if left untreated. Each morning for a week Mary turned up at the clinic prepared for emergency surgery, with an empty stomach and an overnight bag, before going to work after the check-up as if nothing were wrong. Finally a heartbeat showed up on the scan, but their celebrations, like the tiny life, were short-lived. Mary had a miscarriage at ten weeks.

The sixth cycle had been different. The clinic staff surprised the couple by offering to transfer back three blastocysts, unusual because of guidelines aimed at reducing multiple births. The decision to stick to two was quickly made. 'Something told me that it would be all or nothing', Roger recalls. Soon Mary started to feel 'odd', and the next few days were punctuated by frequent dizzy spells. As she strolled outside the office after that fateful phone call she understood why. Even then she could not truly believe that she was pregnant until it was confirmed by a scan, but that had to wait until after the Christmas holiday abroad, which they had booked as some compensation for another possible disappointment.

Flying back two weeks later, Mary made the mistake of eating the airline meal. Stomach cramps were followed by vomiting as food poisoning set in, and it was several more days before she was well enough to have the scan. She gasped as she saw two unmistakeable heartbeats. Yes, there really were twins!

On their way out of hospital that summer Mary and Roger called at the infertility unit to show off their two beautiful boys. And of course they took in a photo of two happy babies for the clinic's collection.

Two sisters

Infertility has many causes, and close relatives can have very different experiences

'Megan, is that you?' Megan recognised her sister's voice as she picked up the phone. It was early on Christmas morning. 'I'm pregnant!', Amanda whispered, as she and husband Ken sat in bed staring at the blue line on the pregnancy test. It was their first IVF cycle, and they weren't due to do the test until the following week. But how could they wait that long? This was a perfect family Christmas present. 'Don't tell Mum and Dad', Amanda added, as she wanted to break the happy news to her parents face to face the following day.

Megan and Amanda had always been close. Yet Megan had struggled with guilt when she found out that she was expecting her second child, because she knew the heartache her sister was experiencing. She already had one child, and she had also become pregnant easily on the second occasion, whereas Amanda and Ken had been trying for a child without success for a long time before they were referred for treatment. They were both investigated, and IVF was prescribed after Ken's low sperm count had been pinpointed.

As a doctor Megan was familiar with IVF, and the associated risk of multiple pregnancies. She knew that two five-day-old embryos, or blastocysts, had been implanted into Amanda, so that twins were a definite possibility. And not long afterwards Amanda proudly announced that she was indeed expecting twins. A blood test had confirmed the pregnancy, and a subsequent scan revealed two babies, alive and well, pulsating blobs on the screen which Amanda and Ken referred to as their 'little squirrels'.

Amanda's twin pregnancy was a much more clinical experience than Megan, despite her medical training, had imagined, in comparison to her own with single babies. The regular scans and blood tests, and the unrelenting medical attention, although reassuring, also created anxiety. Everything seemed to be black and white, with no shades of grey, and the cold numbers in which the results from various tests were reported added no colour. Even the terms 'twin one' and 'twin two' used by the doctors had an

32

unsettling ring. Keen to personalise their babies, Amanda and Ken wanted to know their sexes, finding out at sixteen weeks that they were a boy and a girl. 'One of each, how perfect!', Megan commented.

Amanda was delighted when Dylan and Sarah were delivered by planned Caesarean section at week 38, each weighing 2.3 kg (5 lb). She was even more delighted, and very surprised, to find herself naturally pregnant only a few months later, so that the age gap between her twins and her third child would be just fifteen months. Although it seems like an improbable twist in a complicated television plot, the vagaries of infertility still retain the capacity to surprise, and her experience is far from unique.

Repeat order

IVF first time round usually means IVF again for a second child

The phone call to the infertility clinic was a half-hearted attempt to revive plans for a second child. 'I'm thinking of coming in again', Wendy explained. There was, she was told, a slot for IVF treatment the following month, due to an unexpected cancellation. After mulling it over briefly she called back, and within two weeks the process had started.

'Everything was wonderful with our first child', Wendy explains. She and her husband had finally settled in one town after several years of moving, and they were at last able to focus on their future. But their tries for a baby were unsuccessful, so they were interested to hear of a new IVF procedure. Known as ICSI, this involved a single sperm being injected into an egg, and the success rates were promising, although it was still in its infancy. They decided to give it a go.

The initial consultations were in their home town, but the eggs would be harvested and the embryos implanted at a London clinic. The cost was crippling, so they were quite happy when an early scan confirmed a twin pregnancy. Buy one, get one free. Unfortunately their elation evaporated when, at eleven weeks, there was just one heartbeat to be seen. They had lost one of their babies. After this unsettling start, followed by an anxious pregnancy, they were relieved when Ethan was born, even though he was six weeks early. They had, after all, got the one healthy baby they were originally seeking.

That had been success at their first IVF attempt, but this beginners' luck didn't last, and the next pregnancy ended with a miscarriage. Wendy had agreed to donate surplus eggs from her treatment to other couples, giving them the opportunity to become parents. 'I would have accepted somebody else's eggs, so why wouldn't I give them my own?' It was some consolation to hear that there had been a 'good success rate' with her donated eggs.

Ethan was three by the time Wendy summoned up the courage to make that phone call to the clinic. The quick appointment was followed by early success, and at six weeks a single heartbeat in a single sac was visible on the scan. Ethan's insistence that there would be two baby boys was countered by Wendy's patient explanation: 'No, mummies only have one baby at a time.' Despite feeling quite different this time around, she never suspected twins. She was wearing maternity clothes as early as nine weeks, felt quite unwell and was plagued by a persistent pain in her pelvis, but these potential signs of a multiple pregnancy were ignored. The evidence indicated a single embryo, until at the twelve-week scan the sonographer saw identical twins sharing the same sac and placenta. Ethan said to his tearful mother: 'See. I told you. It's two!'

Wendy was very much aware of how precarious her previous pregnancies had been. Perhaps the twins, if they survived, would be premature. There were practicalities to consider, and the cost of raising three young children loomed large after expensive IVF. By week fourteen doctors had diagnosed pregnancy-related diabetes. Suddenly Wendy was watching her food, taking insulin and making repeated visits to the clinic. She was determined to give her babies a good head start. 'When you're carrying a precious cargo, you look after yourself.'

Getting pregnant on holiday

'IVF tourism' provides a new twist to an old cliché

Looking overseas for IVF treatment is becoming increasingly popular, although many doctors remain wary about the varying standards of care in some countries. The reasons people have for going abroad also vary. Some are looking for cheaper options than are available in the UK, particularly if they do not qualify for free NHS treatment or have used up their quota of free attempts. Others may target countries with fewer restrictions on the permitted number of embryos implanted, hoping to increase their chances of success – and their risk of a multiple pregnancy. Some couples favour a relaxed environment, mixing the business of baby-making with the pleasure of a sunny holiday. Clinics in idyllic locations promise turquoise seas and dazzling white beaches, offering them as the perfect back-drop for supposedly stress-free IVF.

Sandra had not anticipated the struggle she would have to conceive a third child, following two trouble-free pregnancies. Eventually she was referred to the infertility clinic at the local hospital, where she was prescribed Clomid, a drug designed to stimulate her ovaries to produce the follicles containing eggs. This would be followed by intra-uterine insemination (IUI), the injection of her partner's sperm directly into her uterus. She responded well to the treatment, indeed too well. The doctors discovered that too many follicles had developed, so that the risk of a higher-order multiple pregnancy (triplets or more) was too great.

Instead of the planned insemination, the medical team then decided to carry out an egg collection, the procedure used in IVF. However only four eggs were retrieved from eight healthy follicles, and just two of these matured sufficiently for the next stage. Sperm was mixed with the eggs, but sadly neither was fertilised. With hindsight, Sandra was disappointed that the staff had not suggested ICSI, a technique whereby a single sperm is injected directly into the egg, which is used with good results in IVF.

The family had a re-think, during which a friend with a multiple pregnancy recommended an IVF clinic in Poland. The whole package, including travel costs, would be cheaper than private treatment in the UK, and they hoped for better results too. The clinic offered ICSI as a matter of course, and was fully staffed seven days a week. Impressed by reports of the high standard of care and intense monitoring throughout the process, Sandra enrolled. 'In the Polish clinic the whole focus was on getting pregnant', she notes. During her treatment she was required to attend the clinic each morning, and she spent the afternoons exploring the city. On the key day her partner flew over from the UK to provide the vital sperm sample, and they were both overjoyed to learn soon afterwards that this single IVF cycle had produced the desired pregnancy. That the eventual result turned out to be twin girls was an added bonus.

But that was not the last surprise. Only a couple of years later Sandra became pregnant again, this time naturally.

Upgraded to twins

It wasn't quite the mile-high club, but Sarah got pregnant on an aeroplane (well, almost)

Sarah drifted in and out of a half-sleep. Just as she was about to nod off, the piercing cry of yet another young child would rouse her. 'We're sitting in the nursery!', George had exclaimed after boarding their aeroplane at Los Angeles, bound for London. They were just grateful for these last two seats on the overbooked flight, and the minor inconvenience of noisy children would soon fade. But not for long.

After several unsuccessful attempts at IVF, George and Sarah had indulged themselves with a three-week around-the-world tour. Staff at the clinic had given Sarah the nasal spray needed for the first stage of a new cycle, so that she could begin using it if her period started while she was still abroad. Inevitably it did – in the Australian outback. Following the complicated IVF timetable was tricky enough without the added problem of time zones. What time had it had been in London? Having changed her watch three times in one week, jet lag prevented clear thinking. Finally she phoned the clinic and was given a date and time for taking the first dose.

As the crowded jumbo jet taxied out for takeoff at Los Angeles, Sarah reminded herself that she was due to start the medication that night, and she had carefully packed the nasal spray in her hand luggage. The clinic had given her a precise time to use the spray, but that was London time. After shifting across so many different time-zones and crossing the international date-line just 24 hours previously, she wasn't entirely sure of the day, let alone the time.

Finally she conceded defeat. As the cabin lights dimmed, she gave up calculating and just took the medication in the hope that it would work. And it did. As Sarah and George stepped off the plane in London, they had already embarked on a course of treatment that would change their own lives. And create another two. They had been upgraded in more ways than one that night.

Twins squared

Delivering one set of twins is challenging; delivering a second set is remarkable

Early in Debbie's first pregnancy Kevin twice dreamt that there were two babies. 'There aren't any twins in my family', she assured him, yet at the twelve-week scan two heartbeats were clearly visible. Shocked yet happy, she knew that they would manage. The pregnancy passed without any complications, and she remained in good health, working in a hairdressing salon until the thirty-fifth week. 'All I could do was waddle around, taking every opportunity to rest. My stomach grew daily.' At week 36 her waters broke and she was admitted to hospital, where her fourteen-hour labour was 'pretty average' before Rachel was born, at 3.1 kg (6 lb 12 oz).

Then everything ground to a halt, as the contractions ceased. Twin two was still encased in the unbroken amniotic sac and showed no signs of distress, so Debbie was given medication to re-commence the labour. The atmosphere remained relaxed, with the midwife chatting to Kevin as they waited for the drugs to take effect. A Caesarean section would only be performed if the second baby had not appeared within two hours of the first.

The delivery suite was busy that night, and another expectant mother of twins was also experiencing difficulties. The consultant could only hope that he would not have to decide which babies to retrieve first, as his overstretched team was unable to perform two Caesarean sections on twins at the same time. Debbie remained calm, although casting longing glances over to new-born Rachel, who lay quietly in her cot under a heat lamp, but she knew that she had to focus on the second baby. The consultant was becoming increasingly concerned as the two hours elapsed, knowing that surgery would soon be required. A sudden drop in the baby's heartbeat caused alarm, but happily a false alarm, as the monitor had merely slipped and was failing to pick up the palpitations. Perhaps it was this which motivated Debbie to get the baby out, so she pushed and Daniel was born, weighing 3.0 kg (6 lb 11 oz).

Debbie's energy seemed boundless, and she set up her own business as a mobile hairdresser, arriving at clients' houses with her equipment, playpen and two babies. She adored her twins, but raising them did seem to have been a non-stop treadmill of feeding, nappies and other tasks. She intended to have another child, but looking at friends who had been able to devote their energies to their single babies, she now wanted what she saw as the easy option. It would be great just to carry her child without a buggy, rather than juggling babies and belongings like a circus act. It never occurred to her that she might have twins again.

She became pregnant quickly, and this time she felt much more sick and tired. Suspecting the pregnancy was not a straightforward one, she requested an early scan at eight weeks. With her eyes glued to the screen she explained why she was there. 'There's nothing wrong with me, but I just need you to tell me there's only one baby in there.' The sonographer's response was like a slap in the face. 'You're not going to like this.' Debbie burst into tears as she saw the fluttering image of double heartbeats on the screen.

Despite the shock, the second pregnancy caused little trouble. Debbie felt bigger, but in photos the bump appeared to be the same size. This time she found walking difficult towards the end, as well as being plagued by tiredness. And of course she had two young children to add to her burden.

At week 36 a scan showed that twin one was lying across her belly, so a Caesarean section was arranged for week 38, but on arrival at the hospital Debbie insisted on a scan beforehand. She had already experienced a vaginal delivery, and she hoped to avoid surgical intervention this time. 'Birth should be a natural event. Babies are supposed to be born that way.' She recalls how as a young child her mother had waved her good-bye at the school gate one day, only to turn up at the end of the afternoon with the washing on the line, the household chores completed and a new baby. All in a day's work.

The scan confirmed that twin one had moved again, this time into the correct position, and Debbie's labour had already started. Her sole concern was for the babies, and this time she was not going to allow a two-hour gap between them. As she paced restlessly around the ward she suddenly felt the urge to push, just managing to get back to her bed before calling for help. There was no time to lose, and Kevin and the midwife dragged her unceremoniously into the delivery room, with Debbie loudly insisting: 'I'm going to have the baby any moment!' Kevin rushed back to collect her bags, reappearing just as Naomi was born, weighing 3.3 kg (7 lb 3 oz).

Suddenly a host of midwives and doctors bustled in, as if late for an important meeting. It was the shift change, so there were two sets of staff present. Debbie felt reassured, but there was no chance of rest as the doctors pressed on her stomach to prevent the second baby from turning. They broke her waters and encouraged her to push. Another healthy 2.8 kg (6 lb 3 oz) girl, Thea, was born 29 minutes later. After just two more days the family were all together again at home.

In for the long haul

Surely you mean ten hours in the delivery suite, not ten days?

Sitting on the toilet in the middle of the night, Sonya let out a gasp. Her waters had suddenly come gushing out, and at week 31 it was too soon. But there was no mistake. This was it. Hastily getting dressed, she and husband Greg grabbed the bag that had stood at the ready since week 29, leaped into the car, and headed for the conveniently nearby maternity hospital, a towel jammed between her legs to soak up the continuing flow of liquid.

A brief examination confirmed that twin one's waters had broken, and that labour was imminent. There was more bad news. The hospital was equally unprepared for the unexpected development, and the necessary two intensive-care premature baby cots were not available in Oxford. Sonya's heart sank as she realised that she would have to be transferred to another hospital. But where? The search widened as one hospital after another confirmed that they had one, but not two cots free. Birmingham, Southampton, London and Bristol were all tried, and Cardiff and even Newcastle were being mentioned before Luton finally came up trumps two hours later. A dramatic hour-long ambulance ride followed, in the small hours and – appropriately, it seemed – in pouring rain, although prosaically punctuated by roadside toilet stops. Greg followed in the car, gloomily wondering whether the people who analyse traffic camera photographs might guess why he was hard on the tail of a speeding ambulance.

In the cold light of a Luton dawn, a doctor explained that the majority of babies are born within 24 hours of the waters breaking, and that all arrive within three days. The nursery was yet to decorate and even the cots were still to buy, so Greg returned to Oxford later that day. But not for long. Sonya's contractions started at 3 a.m. the next morning, although it was 8.30 a.m. by the time she was transferred to the delivery suite, occupied until then by the arrival of another set of even more premature twins. Labour was confirmed, with contractions every five minutes, and an anaesthetist quickly administered an epidural to numb the pain. But then nothing happened, as although the contractions continued no twins made their appearance.

Two days later Sonya was still hooked up to an array of monitors, with contractions gripping her body every few minutes, and the doctors were divided as to how to deal with this exceptional situation. All were agreed that it was in the interests of the babies' long-term health for them to stay in the womb as long as possible, but was this feasible, even though twin two's waters had not broken and he was still reasonably snug in his sac? Sonya had coped well so far, but she also had an underlying health problem, and there were ominous signs of urinary difficulties developing. A junior doctor felt that a Caesarean section was necessary, and some of his senior colleagues were inclined to agree with him, until the issue was resolved by the return to duty of Sonya's own consultant, breezily announcing, but in a tone of voice which clearly expected no dissent: 'So we're going for a natural delivery, aren't we?'

Soon a routine was established, with Greg alternating between Oxford by day preparing the home for the new arrivals, and back in Luton for the night with Sonya in the delivery suite. Constant monitoring deprived her of sleep, but at least the babies were doing well inside her body. After four days she decided to wash her hair, waiting until the doctor had finished his rounds before hobbling to the sink in the delivery suite and liberally sprinkling her head with antiseptic hand-wash. It was a tricky business, with a large protruding bump, an epidural drip and a urinary catheter to cope with.

After five days the contractions slowed down to twenty-minute intervals, and Sonya, with her squeaky clean hair, was transferred back to the labour ward. Again not for long, as they soon speeded up, so it was back to the now-familiar delivery suite, where the waiting game continued. All romantic notions of the 'happy event' had long since been dispelled, and the birth plan had been filed in the fiction section. Then after an early-morning examination the consultant announced that pushing could commence. It was soon evident that the epidural had worn off, as the patient requested the consultant anaesthetist in quaint Anglo-Saxon to top up the pain-relief. 'Nothing can prepare you for that level of eye-popping pain. It was twin one, and I knew I had another one to go.'

In an attempt to take her mind off the ordeal, Sonya busied herself counting the occupants of the little room. She reached 21, comprising various doctors (including one lurking ominously with a set of forceps), two resuscitation teams, one for each baby, with their high-tech equipment, plus midwives, nurses and a group of student midwives, not to mention her husband. Finally Eric was born, by now in week 33, and after a quick cuddle and a pee on the floor he was whisked off to the neonatal unit by the team assigned to him. Concerned that twin two's heartbeat had been lost on the monitor, the staff made preparations for an emergency dash to the operating theatre for a Caesarean, but fortunately the pulsating signals were picked up again. The baby's waters were broken artificially after a final ultrasound scan showed that he was head down in the right direction, and eventually Peter was born, 32 minutes after his brother. Anxious staff whisked him away to the neonatal unit even before his mother could see him.

Eleven days after starting out, Sonya lay shaking with exhaustion in the near-empty room. 'They *were* both boys, weren't they?', she enquired. Then photos appeared, with the welcome message from the neonatal unit that both were doing well. Eric, who had been managing on only a trickle of amniotic fluid for the duration, was 1.8 kg (3lb 15 oz), and Peter tipped the scales at 2.0 kg (4lb 8 oz). Sonya soon recovered her strength, and busied herself looking after the new men in her life.

She scored twice ...
but her husband got the medal

**There is more than one way into the world, but usually both
twins take the same route**

Her pregnancy had progressed well, and Sally was aiming for a
natural birth. In both her previous labours in her native New
Zealand she had been induced after her waters had broken, but
while daughter Matisse required a Caesarean section, her sister
Italia was born naturally. Now, on the other side of the world in
South Wales with her professional rugby-player husband Filo, she
hoped to do it that way again, even though this time it was twins.

At week 37 she started to show symptoms of pre-eclampsia, so
that an early delivery was required. Sally was keen enough to be
induced for a natural birth, as her body felt stretched to capacity,
but she was astounded when the consultant recommended a
Caesarean section, as twin one was in the breech position (bottom
first). She had seen the scan, and she knew that the presenting twin
was in fact head-down. After re-reading the notes, the consultant
checked with the sonographer, who realised that he had muddled
the twins up. Twin one was indeed head-down and ready to go, so
Sally could be induced. 'Can you come in tomorrow?', the doctor
asked in a matter-of-fact manner. 'I guess so', she muttered, already
preoccupied with thoughts of how to make such last-minute
arrangements for the care of her older girls.

After the induction next morning the contractions soon started,
but the labour did not progress. On the following day Sally was
induced again, but there was no noticeable response to the drugs,
although contractions continued. With two children at home who
also needed her, she started to feel anxious about the lengthy
labour and frustrated by the changes of staff as shifts came and
went. 'I felt that there was no one batting for me.' Reluctantly she
stayed in hospital for a second night, while Filo went home to the
older girls.

On the third morning the consultant explained the alternatives.
They could either wait for nature to take its course, or he could
speed things up by breaking Sally's waters surgically. She opted
for the latter, so Filo pushed her to the delivery suite in a

wheelchair, with her bags on a trolley alongside. Then, expecting another long wait, he went off to eat. All being well, he was due to play in an important match the next day, and he had to follow his prescribed training diet. When he returned he was shocked to find his wife in full-blown labour, although an internal examination indicated that there was still a long way to go. Just as the anaesthetist was explaining how the epidural would work, Sally murmured, almost to herself: 'It's there!', but nobody caught her words. Then the midwife noticed. 'The baby's coming. Move your leg or you'll squash its head!' Within minutes baby Gianna emerged, Filo cut the umbilical cord, and the midwife presented the little girl to her mother.

Sally was still having contractions, but her earlier apprehension about giving birth twice in a row had disappeared. Gianna's arrival had been so smooth and easy. Even a move to the operating theatre did not concern her, as it was only so that the second baby could be manipulated into the head-down delivery position. Then little Emina poked out an arm, making a vaginal delivery too risky. The team had to act quickly, and there was no time to wait for an epidural to take effect, so Sally needed a general anaesthetic. Filo had to go, reluctantly, as he had been present at Matisse's Caesarean section delivery under epidural, but this time there was no room for spectators. The next thing that Sally remembers was waking to find that she had two healthy 2.7 kg (6 lb) babies, born just thirty minutes apart, but already in their short lives having had quite different experiences of the world.

Filo left the hospital that evening, and early the following morning he was driven to London's Twickenham rugby ground, where the rest of his team, the Ospreys, were already assembled to play in the final of the EDF Energy Cup. The opposition, the formidable Leicester Tigers, seemed none too pleased to see the equally formidable Filo, the 1.92 m and 112 kg All Black, (6' 4" and 17½ stone), as he ran out onto the famous turf. 'There was every chance that he would have missed the game, had things worked out differently', a club spokesman later commented. The Ospreys won a comfortable 23-6 victory, with Filo putting in one of his most redoubtable performances. His comment: 'It was the perfect weekend for me, with two beautiful new daughters and a cup winner's medal into the bargain.'

Taken by surprise

Like guests who arrive too early for dinner, premature babies sometimes get an uncertain welcome

'It's April Fool's Day', had been Helen's first thought when the sonographer said that the scan showed twins. But the midwife *had* already noted that she was big for her expected delivery date, although as this was her first pregnancy she had known no different. By week 29 she suspected that something was going wrong. She explained to the consultant that sitting down felt as if she were squashing a baby's head. Maybe the babies were ready to be born? Two days later she woke at five in the morning and noticed that the bed was wet. The second time, two hours later, she rang the hospital to explain that she kept wetting herself. Was it significant? The midwife asked her to come in, although it was probably nothing and she would soon be home again.

By eight Helen was getting sharp twinges, and an examination confirmed that labour was under way. Twin one's head was far enough down to act as a plug, stopping the broken waters gushing out of the birth canal and leaving only a thin trickle. She was given a steroid injection to help the premature babies' lungs develop, but after she brought up the tablets she had taken to delay labour the doctor ominously pronounced: 'These babies are coming today!'

He was right. Suddenly there were eighteen people in the room. In a whirlwind of activity staff prepared beds in the neonatal unit and cots with resuscitation equipment in the delivery suite. Helen panicked. Her antenatal classes were not scheduled until the following week! An epidural needle was inserted into her back, but the twins made their appearances before the anaesthetic could take effect, so she had to settle for gas and air. Chloe arrived at 2.08 p.m., and was put straight into a waiting incubator and wheeled off. Two minutes later Charlotte was born, still encased in her amniotic sac, causing husband Simon to quip: 'It's been born in a carrier bag!' The medical team knowingly took a step back as the sac was pierced, while Simon got soaked. 'It's good luck to be born in the amniotic sac', commented a midwife, after baby Charlotte had been whisked off to join her sister.

Helen went into shock. Nine hours ago she had been pregnant, with eleven more weeks to go. Now she had two tiny premature babies, although she had neither seen them nor held them yet. How could she bond with them? She didn't dare to ask how they were faring, as she wanted to keep them at a distance in case they didn't pull through. Simon visited the little twins, finding them surrounded by a maze of tubes in their incubators, where they were being ventilated as they were unable to breathe by themselves. He showed Helen the snapshots which had been taken in the neonatal unit, renewing her panic at the thought that this might have been done because they were going to die. (In fact it is standard practice to give photos of premature babies to their parents if they cannot be with them.)

Early the next morning Helen was taken to see her daughters for the first time. She was confronted by two tiny babies, with translucent skin, like birds with no feathers, and hooked up to a daunting array of monitors. Charlotte was still being ventilated, and at 1.1 kg (2 lb 6 oz) she was slightly smaller than Chloe, 1.2 kg (2 lb 10 oz). The experience was very clinical, and Helen continued to resist the urge to become too attached to the babies in case their tiny lives ebbed away. A couple of days later she at last got to hold them. 'It was the most terrifying thing I'd ever done.' How different this was to those babies with their mothers on the maternity ward, whose blankets were decorated with ribbons rather than oxygen tubes.

Helen functioned like a robot, excelling at the practicalities of looking after the babies without acknowledging them to herself as her own. It was not until much later, when the twins were moved out of the high dependency unit into the hospital nursery, that she allowed herself to fall in love with her girls. 'We knew then that we were on the home stretch.'

Two's too many

Before ultrasound scans, the second twin was sometimes a complete surprise

The two women in their early seventies sunning themselves on the deck of the pleasure steamer on Berlin's expansive Wannsee lake were clearly enjoying each other's company. Noting their obvious interest in my toddler twin boys, despite the language difference, I looked more closely. They did appear very similar. We got talking, and they told me their own and their mother's story.

Eva had smiled with delight as she held her firstborn child. There were so many things she would show to little Irene as she grew up. Yet Eva's belly remained large, the contractions continued, and her face still looked drawn from the symptoms of pre-eclampsia. The midwife was first anxious, then incredulous. 'There is another baby!' There had never been any mention of twins, and ultrasound scanning did not exist in 1939. Five arduous hours later Christine emerged, a healthy identical twin to her older sister.

The shock was too much for Eva, and she spent the next three years in a sanatorium. The little girls were looked after separately, Irene by her grandmother and Christine by her father, although they saw each other frequently. They were not finally reunited with their mother until after their third birthday. Eva loved Irene, the child she had longed for, whereas she struggled to accept Christine as a part of her family, even though the girls looked so alike. For a long time she could not disguise her bitter feelings towards the second twin, whose unexpected arrival had thrown her life off balance. As the trippers admired Potsdam's palaces from the passing boat, Christine's voice wavered as she relived the sense of rejection she grew up with.

In March 1945, just weeks before the end of the Second World War, the girls' father was killed in an Allied air raid on the Berlin aircraft factory where he had been working. The six-year-old girls were left with only their mother, who was finally forced to acknowledge them both as her daughters, bringing them successfully through the hard post-war years in the devastated city. They remained a close-knit family until Eva's death, which had occurred twelve years previously.

Coincidentally both Irene and Christine have grown-up twin grandchildren, yet they recognise that the bond between these boy-girl fraternal pairs is not as strong as their own relationship as identical twins. That was further cemented after Christine was diagnosed with cancer, yet fortunately she enjoys good health in remission. Her illness helped them to appreciate how important they are to each other. 'We realise that we belong together. We are like a mother to each other.' They both nodded in agreement.

Easy peasy

After twins, delivering a single baby would be easy ...

In the delivery room Corinna recalled the arrival of her twin boys two years previously. Then her waters had broken seven weeks early, heralding their imminent arrival, and the high-speed ambulance ride to the hospital had stirred distressing memories of an earlier car crash, and the air ambulance which had flown her to safety. Nevertheless she had been quite composed, sure that the birth of the babies would not be traumatic.

Odd though it may seem, the emergency Caesarean section had been a tranquil experience. The pain relief was effective, enabling Corinna to relax and take in all that was going on. Husband Michael had inspired confidence, watching the procedure with great interest and getting a running commentary from the surgical team. He had happily witnessed his children take their first breath, and Laurin and Leon were fit and healthy, each weighing 2.0 kg (4 lb 6 oz), so that they could leave hospital after just one week.

Now it was different. 'Get a move on! The baby's going to die!' The doctor's sharp words jolted her back to the present, where the expected easy delivery of her singleton third child was going badly wrong. A full medical team stood primed to receive and revive the traumatised baby, and the pressure was on Corinna to push him out quickly. He was five weeks premature, and with a rising sense of panic she feared that she was going to lose her child. Then, quite suddenly, Linus emerged, and the room was filled with the welcome sound of a crying baby. As he filled his lungs with air there were sighs of relief from staff and parents, and the doctor quietly apologised for his forceful but clearly effective words, unscripted in the birth plan.

The problem had started with a searing pain which Corinna had experienced during the delivery, caused by the placenta coming away from the womb. Known as placenta abrupta, this condition is potentially life-threatening to the baby and occasionally to the mother too. Every moment counts, and the swift delivery of baby Linus had saved his life. Today this terror-stricken birth is all but forgotten, as the spirited 'three musketeers' band of brothers romp uproariously around their home.

What parents say

'It's double the love, and it's also double the crying and the screaming, so it's a unique blessed situation.' (*P. Diddy, singer and father of twins*)

'Twins are hard work. They're twice the amount of work, but also twice the love and twice the fun.' (*Jennifer Lopez, actress, singer and mother of twins*)

'It takes more time, but it's no harder than a singleton. It's lovely.' (*Jo, mother of twins and of a single child*)

'It was worth it in the end.' (*Caroline, mother of newborn twin boys*)

'My first children were just ten months apart, and worn out by two consecutive pregnancies and having small babies to look after, I would tell friends that this is what it is like to have twins. Several years later I really did have twins. It was only then that I realised just how different it is, requiring so much more energy. I wasn't at all prepared for it.' (*Holly, mother of twins and two older children*)

'I found the baby stage hard, perhaps even horrendous!' (*Pam, mother of twins and an older child*)

'I have a twin sister, and I had non-identical twins twenty years ago. There is nothing special about twins, just a lot of very hard work.' (*Jennifer*)

'There is so much more work involved with twins than I had ever imagined.' (*Rachel, mother of twins and an older child*)

'The health visitor asked me whether I could distinguish the cries of each baby. From that moment on I realised that they were individuals, and not part of a package. I used to amaze other mothers in baby groups by immediately recognising which of my two was crying, and tending to their needs.' (*Millie, mother of twins*)

'My husband is at work all day, and I am used to dealing with the babies by myself. You must be really organised, which can be quite tiring. You have to deal with two children, often trying to meet their needs at the same time, which isn't always possible. At least they have slept through the night from four months old, so I can get the sleep that I need.' (*Susanne, mother of one-year-old twins and a teenage girl*)

'With the second set, I didn't worry about favouring one twin over the other. I expected to feel different at different times, depending on the situation. Being fair doesn't mean treating them the same, rather it means reacting to the circumstances as appropriate.' (*Debbie, mother of two sets of young twins*)

'My friend with three young children was keen to help, but I soon realised that her well-meant advice didn't apply to twins.' (*Jennie, mother of twins*)

'On moving abroad with the young babies, I bought a parenting book to brush up on my baby-speak in the local language. I soon realised I was going it alone when the only advice to parents of twins, right at the end, was to ignore everything in the book and to work out a routine from first principles. Life became easier after that.' (*Jennie, mother of twins*)

'On my early outings with Lionel I would worry that I had forgotten something. It took a while to realise that leaving the house with supplies for just one baby was much easier than it had been with the twins.' (*Connie, mother of twins and a new baby*)

'I've been sleeping like a baby. I sleep two hours, wake up and cry. Sleep two hours, wake up and cry.' (*John McCain, explaining in a television interview how he had coped the week after losing his fight with Barack Obama for the American presidency. McCain is not the father of twins, but ex-President George W. Bush is, and doubtless knows even more about crying babies.*)

Leave it to Auntie

Looking after twins is quite different from coping with one at a time

Jayne realised that Mandy needed a rest. 'We'll look after the twins for a couple of hours while you relax', she confidently promised her sister, who was visiting with her six-week-old twins. Mandy was exhausted and more than ready to fall into bed until it was time for the ten-o-clock feed, so she disappeared upstairs.

Jayne and her husband Tim were sure that they could look after their niece and nephew, as they were themselves experienced parents, with a four-year-old boy and a four-month-old baby. Then twin Sarah started to whimper. Suddenly they were faced with a new dilemma. Dealing for the first time with two babies of the same age, they would have to make a decision which took both into account. Should they leave Sarah and risk her waking brother Daniel, or should they go in and comfort her, and risk waking Daniel that way? If she had been a single baby, they would have left her to cry for a while, hoping that she would fall asleep. They were so much more relaxed with their second baby than they had been with their first child, yet now they were hesitant and uncertain.

They decided to leave her, hoping that she would wear herself out before she woke her brother. It was the wrong decision. Soon both babies were awake, and the air was resonant with screams from their tiny lungs. The cries became more urgent, and Auntie Jayne detected a note of hysteria in her charges. Finally she and Tim took the babies out of their cots and tried to calm them down. They each held one baby, yet the twins were beyond soothing. With growing panic Jayne wondered how her sister could comfort both babies at the same time, all by herself. How was that possible? Eventually she conceded defeat, and she and Tim slunk up to Mandy's room to wake her and hand the two little ones back to their mother, as nothing else would pacify them.

This small incident started to bring home to Jayne what it meant to have twins. 'It was a real eye-opener. It's not just twice as much work; it's a higher multiple than that.' Her sister's life seemed to be a daily juggling act. Jayne had let her own babies fall into their natural feeding and sleeping patterns, but with two it was quite different. Mandy had to decide whether to feed them both at the same time, or whether to let the babies set their own schedule according to their body clocks. If one woke up, should she rouse the other and feed them both? If not, she risked the second twin waking just as she was ready to fall back into bed at four o'clock in the morning. But is it cruel to wake a baby to feed? Or is getting through the first difficult weeks, by whatever means, all that matters? Just one or two of the many questions posed by life with new twins, Jayne realised.

Feeding-time talk

'We quickly settled into a routine at the hospital. The twins were born early, at week 33, but without any health complications. Feeding them through a nasal-gastric tube was an art we soon mastered, and was remarkably easy. They thrived on a mixture of breast and formula milk. Soon they were strong enough to take just my milk from the breast and the bottle, and they relished both.' (*Jill, mother of premature twins*)

'I loved breast-feeding the twins. It helped me to bond with them, but I had to eat constantly as I was permanently hungry!' (*Jo, mother of twin baby boys and an older toddler*)

'The only way to pacify my babies at my nephew's christening was to bring along a friend to cuddle one baby while I fed the other, and then to swap them over. Before the church service an admirer from my teenage years turned around to say hello, just as eight-month-old Emily was latching on. Enjoying the distraction, she turned her head towards my old flame, leaving my cumbersome boob exposed with a jet of milk squirting out which just missed his face. I could have died.' (*Lisa, mother of twins*)

'I was determined to give my boys breast milk, and our routine involved me feeding them myself and also expressing my own milk for bottles for my husband to do the night feed. At three months we took the children on a long car journey to visit their newborn cousin. I decided against tandem feeding at the motorway service station, where a coach-load of male football supporters was sitting near us, so instead I took the electric double breast-pump into the baby change area. As I stood there revealing all, with a bottle held to each breast accompanied by the whirring noise of the machine, a male cleaner came in. He stood rooted to the spot, like a frightened rabbit caught in the headlights, before quickly scuttling off, and he didn't reappear.' (*Claire, mother of twins*)

'It's scary taking two babies home from hospital. If one cries, the other joins in. How do you pacify two screaming newborns?' Fiona soon learned to breast-feed both babies at the same time, but not in public. 'Tandem feeding is never discreet, unlike feeding one baby at a time.' She recalls seeing a picture of a bold mother feeding both twins in a pub garden, but 'although I admired her bravery, I still think that feeding twins isn't for public viewing!' (*Fiona, mother of two sets of twins, aged six and one*)

After moving to Berlin, away from her family and her native Bavaria, Claudia had to be independent with her twins from the outset. Bottles were the ideal solution, and the boys moved on from expressed to formula milk. 'Breast-feeding in public was out of the question for me. No one gave the twins a second glance being fed bottles, but lifting my shirt to feed both babies might have raised an eye-brow or two on public transport.' (*Claudia, mother of twins and a younger baby*)

'By six months I was still feeding the twins myself, and they were growing fast. One evening my husband and I went out to a smart restaurant for a four-course meal, but the portions were rather modest. After ploughing my way through five baskets of bread, I felt that I had to explain to the waitress why I was eating so much. She laughed and said that her brothers were twins. I felt less self-conscious tucking into my second helping of pudding!' (*Jemma, mother of twins*)

'Keen to impress my visiting mother, I invited her to tea at a rather smart coffee house. I had hoped we would slip in unnoticed, but after two helpful waiters had to carry the double buggy up the steps and inside I sensed that heads had already started to turn. We found a suitable table, and I began to feed the children their lunch, whilst sipping my tea from a fine bone china cup and nibbling on simply divine chocolate cake. The twins were grumpy, not happy about staying strapped into the pushchair, and they were not terribly focused on eating. As I was offering the one another mouthful of green, lumpy spinach and pasta from the jar, the other distracted my attention, just as Thomas swept his hand up and knocked the spoon flying. As if in slow motion I watched the contents somersault through the air, narrowly missing a lady's expensive designer jacket at the next table, before landing on the silky flock wallpaper. Diving in to wipe the green goo off the walls, I realised we had outstayed our welcome, so we quickly paid and left.' (*Jess, mother of toddler twins*)

Stung by curiosity

Premature twins can be mini-celebrities, even to celebrities

I wasn't prepared for the attention we received when I went out with my tiny babies. On one occasion I was surrounded by a dozen staff in a large department store. It has never been so easy to get served, before or since. The most memorable occasion was when the boys were one month old. With another three weeks before their official due date they were still small, weighing approximately 2.5 kg (5 lb 8 oz). As we strolled through the park near our home in Oxford one afternoon, the babies were slumbering in the summer heat. A couple and their teenage daughter who were coming the other way split up to make room on the path for our twin buggy, and the man passed on my side.

Before my conscious mind had fully taken in the situation, I had already greeted him. 'Hello Sting.'
With all those teenage idol photos indelibly imprinted on my brain, formal recognition was not necessary. Fully expecting the superstar to walk on, I hardly dared to shake his outstretched hand. 'And who are you?", he asked. 'I'm glad you've spoken to us, as we didn't want to disturb you, but we've never seen such tiny twins before, and we'd love a better look.'

Then came the questions, with Sting firing away and his wife, Trudie Styler, providing encouragement.

Sting:	Did you have the babies naturally?
Me:	Yes.
Trudie:	Good girl!
Sting:	Are you feeding the babies yourself?
Me:	Yes.
Trudie:	Good girl!
Sting:	What are their names?
Me:	Umm .....

Looking back, I can hardly believe it. I was so star-struck that I couldn't recall my own children's names. Should I make some up?

Fortunately husband Geoff is more into rugby and hard rock, so he stepped in quickly. 'Edmund and Philip.' With a sinking feeling I could see the next question coming, but I still couldn't answer it. 'Which one is which?', enquired Sting. Again Geoff filled in. After that it got better. The next five minutes were spent chatting about the birth, whether I had been able to produce enough milk for small but hungry twins, and a myriad other details. Then we discussed Sting's forthcoming tour. 'Why don't you bring the twins with you to the Albert Hall?' Not a practical option, unfortunately, but Trudie kindly arranged us guest tickets to a concert in Berlin the following summer.

And then they were gone. A friend later joked: 'It was all worth it, wasn't it?' Well, it was, although not for that reason, but it was a bonus. In addition to two beautiful babies I now had a great story to tell.

Three years later I sat near Trudie at a concert featuring Sting at the Berlin Philharmonie. Introducing myself to her as the mother of the premature babies she had met one summer afternoon in Oxford, she immediately remembered. 'Oh yes, Sting and I often talk about the twins', she responded.

In the limelight

Like real celebrities, parents of young twins find that public attention can be both positive and negative

Sally is used to passers-by staring, as her rugby-player husband Filo is a former All Black and a well-known local figure, so she shrugs off the admiring glances her twins attract. But when the family spent a holiday in Spain, with their two older girls and the six-month-old twins, they were amazed at the reception they received on a day trip to Tangier. In Morocco twins are thought to bring good luck, and the family was overwhelmed by the enthusiasm, quite unlike Britain, where strangers have been known to shake their heads, imagining themselves with the twins, and wondering how they would cope with the work. One woman even eyed the four and asked: 'Are they *all* your children?'

Rachel feels conspicuous when out with her twins, where even in an anonymous London suburb she has become known as 'the lady with the red twin buggy'. People stare at her, making comments, and often impede her progress along the pavement. The twins are the same size and often dressed in pink and blue. Yet passers-by ask the same questions. 'Are they twins? Are they identical?' Then, inevitably: 'You've got your hands full', or 'Double trouble.'

Katie, heavily pregnant and weaving through a crowded exhibition hall with her young twins in a double pushchair, was taken aback by one passer-by's loud comment: 'Doesn't she know about contraception?'

Sarah, not wishing to enter into discussions on the status of her own and her husband's fertility, was always surprised by how many strangers would sidle up and enquire: 'Twins! Are they natural?'

Mary is fed up with passers-by sticking their faces into the buggy, cooing admiringly at her twin boys, both clad in blue: 'What lovely little girls.' Some have even touched the babies before their mother could intervene, as though they were public property.

Charlotte was glad that her uncle adored the twins, but she was less keen on his habit of calling them the 'biological BOGOFs', ('Buy One Get One Free'). 'We spent over £26,000 on IVF so we feel that we paid for them both in full', she adds.

Katrin says: 'I got so fed up with people's negative reactions to my pregnancy that I stopped mentioning that I was expecting twins. One tactless individual even remarked: "I'd shoot myself if I were expecting twins!"'

Jayne finds that having twins is an automatic passport to new friendships. A couple approached her and her husband as they strolled along the local beach with their double buggy, and announced that they too were expecting twins. They have since become firm friends. Jayne puts it down to 'the twin thing', whereby families with twins are often drawn to each other, like fellow members of a club, because of the range of experiences they share.

Twin trauma

The risks that all babies run are magnified when there is another to remember

Fran had spent the morning preparing her twin babies for their first journey out since coming home from hospital. Evan, their older brother, had just turned five, and she had promised to go to the baker's to collect his birthday cake. The family was ready to leave the house on a chilly November morning, when Fran heard a peculiar noise from the pram. Realising with horror that baby Jeremy had turned blue, and that there were bubbles popping out of his mouth, she instinctively grabbed him and ripped off his snowsuit. He had stopped breathing. She rang at once for an ambulance, and between her own terrified screams she managed to administer resuscitation according to the instructions given to her over the telephone.

Desperate to save her son, she watched as Jeremy's tiny chest swelled with each of her breaths, and she pumped his breastbone with her fingertips to encourage his heart to work. Every second was vital. The ambulance arrived within three minutes, followed by a doctor and the police. As the paramedics administered oxygen, blood oozed from the corners of the baby's mouth. She later learned that one of his lungs had collapsed.

Fran was just about to leave for the hospital with the ambulance when a terrible thought struck her. 'Help!', she gasped to the woman police officer. 'There's another baby in the pram!' In the turmoil she had been so concerned about her sick child that she had forgotten about his twin. The officer reassured her. 'I know. Just go!' The police contacted her husband, and he was soon back at home to take charge of the second baby.

Fran's blood-shot eyes testified to the stress, but within a week Jeremy recovered full use of both lungs. He had suffered from reflux, a common condition in babies which is usually harmless. But instead of simply vomiting back some of his milk feed, he had breathed it into his lungs, and this had caused the problems. Today he is a robust small boy, with no lasting ill effects, although the episode will remain forever etched into Fran's memory.

Yet she can still find something to laugh about in her recollections.

Of course Evan's birthday party was cancelled, but she remembers returning to the house to be greeted by the baker's banal telephone message: 'Your Scooby Doo cake is ready to be picked up.'

Nicer than the nick

But new twins can be as stressful as the most demanding of jobs

Sabine progressed swiftly up the career ladder and through the police ranks, becoming a detective chief inspector charged with investigating suspicious deaths. Her case-book reads like a television series: burglary, grievous bodily harm, armed robbery, drug trafficking, rape, manslaughter, suicide and murder. Although work was never dull, it did have its drawbacks. 'At times it was stressful, and I struggled to come to terms with some of the terrible things I witnessed.' Particularly harrowing were cases involving children, a traumatic background for her later role as mother of a young family.

Sebastian was four and Konstantin just two when fraternal twins Patrick and Justus arrived. Sabine and her husband had decided to try for a third child, but their secret hopes for a girl were soon dashed. 'We both laughed as the ultrasound showed twins, and two boys at that!'

The first year with the twins and two other young children was the most demanding. The stress was quite different from that of her earlier police career, but it was no less real for Sabine. 'I remember that at times I didn't know where to start. Change nappies, give bottles, comfort one of the children? The list was endless. Sometimes I was so overstretched that I would sit on a park bench and cry out of sheer exhaustion. Many people think that twins are so cute. A mum has two arms and can hold two children, but it isn't as straightforward as that.' Fortunately her husband and the grandparents were happy to help out. 'Without them I couldn't have done it.'

Due to a chronic illness which has plagued Sabine for many years, she has taken early retirement from the police. 'I don't miss the job. During my time with the CID I saw all the bad things in this world.' Now she can focus on her family. 'It's great fun having four young schoolchildren who are so close in age. They play so well together. We love our boys.'

Can we play quietly, please?

Double trouble! The common twins cliché is often relevant at playtime

On hearing that twin boys had been invited around to play, seven-year-old Sebastian complained to his mother, Tanya: 'I don't want to play with the twins. They always get me into trouble!'

One day Martina's twin toddlers Chris and Stefan were playing on their ride-on toy cars in the garden, until she noticed that it had gone ominously quiet. Rushing out from the kitchen, she found that the children were missing. There was a hole in the hedge, so she hastily investigated the neighbour's garden, but that too was empty. Grabbing her bike, she headed for the street corner, where she asked some passers-by if they had seen two toddlers making off on their toy cars. They pointed towards the town centre, and Martina pedalled after them in a desperate attempt to reach the main road before they did. Too late, but she did arrive in time to watch with horror as the two boys cheerfully held up the traffic as they went over the zebra crossing by the supermarket. Martina's two older children – not twins – had never undertaken any comparable escapade, but twins will egg each other on, often daring to do what singletons will not.

'My twins love playing good cop and bad cop. Then after a day or two in these roles, they swap. I never know where I stand.' (*Mother of twins*)

Wendy was sitting with her older child, who was recovering from a tonsils operation, when she heard a series of strange tapping noises from the living room. Suddenly there was a sound of rushing water, causing her to dash through, thinking that perhaps there had been a flood in the bathroom and that the ceiling might be about to fall on her toddler twins. Instead she saw that the large fish tank had cracked and emptied its contents onto the carpet. The two giggling girls, now cowering under the coffee table, had taken advantage of the few unsupervised moments. Giving a fine example of the way twins both co-operate and compete, they had taken pebbles from a table candle display and used them to practise their aim on the fish tank. Too busy saving the fish, Wendy forgot to tell them off.

Chatting over tea, Cindy did not notice at first that her toddlers and her hosts' three-year-old had disappeared. Dad went to investigate, and found them all in the little boy's bedroom. The toddlers were 'mountaineering' on the bunk bed, while Niklas stood anxiously, back to the wall with arms outspread. 'I'm protecting my posters from the twins', he explained.

Four-year-old Rachel announced to her mother Kim that she no longer liked nursery school, before finally admitting that this was because she had been told off. 'I was climbing on the fence, and I was nearly at the top. But it wasn't me. It was my friend.' The teacher confirmed that the miscreant had been Rachel. Maintaining her defence, the little girl declared: 'It wasn't me. It was someone who looked like me.' Perhaps it had been identical twin sister Hannah after all?

Twin brains working together can often outwit parents. When Libby's boys were four she heard a strange singing sound early one morning. The twins had slipped out of bed, and using their combined strength and ingenuity to pile up chairs they had gained access to the high cupboard where the key-ring was kept. After unlocking first the back door and then the padlock to the garden shed, they had heaved a heavy reel of garden hose upstairs to their bedroom, where she found them singing into each end of the 'green snake' and using it as an intercom between them.

Party poopers

Gatherings with twins can be a bit different

'Henry has never done that!', an exasperated father exclaimed at his little boy's second birthday party. He had made the mistake of inviting twin toddlers to the celebration, and he was amazed at the range of new possibilities for disruption in his flat which their combined efforts could discover.

After a fraternal punch-up among the presents one boy commented dejectedly 'Will he always be my twin? I don't want him to be!'

'The twins' birthdays were always a challenge to make sure that everything was perceived by the children to be fair. After James had burst into tears watching his four-year-old brother win Pass the Parcel, we quickly repeated the game, counting the wrapped layers carefully to ensure that he did not go away empty-handed. It was a stressful moment, but they both enjoyed the day!' (*Sarah*)

There were eight small children in the garden, three-year-old quads, their two slightly older siblings, and visiting five-year-old twins. Both sets of parents watched in amazement as a large gazebo tent suddenly grew multiple little legs and began to career around the lawn. Later one child confessed: 'It was nobody's idea. We all thought of it together.'

'It was always important for us that at their birthday party each twin could enjoy their own individual rendition of *Happy Birthday*, together with their own cake. It was our way of stressing their individuality despite a shared birthday. Much to my annoyance, one of the mothers with a single child who attended their fourth birthday talked loudly over the second singing of the song. Ironically she is now pregnant herself with twins, so perhaps she might get the point in the future.' (*Imogen*)

'As children we always insisted on giving each other a birthday present. Otherwise as twins we would miss out on one important gift. We have only recently stopped swapping presents, but we

70

always make an effort to meet up and celebrate together.' (*Maria, an adult twin*)

Over the canapés Charles asked after his friend William's fiancée. 'How is your other half?', he enquired. 'He's fine', came the response. But William was referring not to his future wife but to his identical twin brother!

Even after many years of living with her octogenarian husband and his identical twin, Jean notes that when one of them peels an orange he will still offer half to his brother. 'It is as though I am not there, and it's just the two of them', she laughs.

On their 80th birthday, triplets Morgan, Idwal and Ivor met up for a family party, but were surprised when the press reported on the gathering. 'We're as close now as when we were little boys, and we help to keep each other young. They wanted to put 240 candles on our cake, and we would have had no trouble blowing them out. We've still got plenty of puff!' (*Morgan, aged 81*)

Highway to hell?

Twins add another dimension to travelling

'Travelling with young twins qualifies a parent for a job in the circus', a woman quipped to her friend, after watching her, bag in one hand, stop a runaway buggy containing one child with her foot while lunging after the fast-disappearing twin with the other hand.

'While visiting Britain I had to take Joseph and Rebecca out on the bus. In our home town the buses have big doors where you just push the buggy straight in, so it came as a shock to find that I would need to negotiate steps and a narrow aisle to get on board. Watched by the driver and passengers, who were clearly not budging to help, I took out one toddler at a time and sat them on the floor. Then I offloaded the nappy bag, before folding the pushchair and struggling with it on to the bus. After buying my ticket, I took the toddlers to the single seat which was free. The man occupying the neighbouring seat was clearly not giving it up, so I spent the journey sitting cross-legged on the floor, propping up a child with each hand to stop them from sliding off the seat. Fellow travellers were more helpful as I got off, but I felt exhausted by the time I had loaded the twins back into their buggy.' (*Sabine*)

'Changing nappies when we were out and about became an art form. In fine weather the top of the car boot made an impromptu change mat as long as you watched that nobody rolled off. When they were quite small I took them one at a time to the toilet at a motorway service station, leaving the other twin with my partner. The attendant standing by the door looked a bit surprised when I reappeared with a second baby. By the time I got back the first twin had filled his nappy again, and she looked distinctly edgy when I arrived with a third identical-looking baby. It brought a smile to my face that day!' (*Mary*)

'Our first trip abroad was on an overnight ferry when the twins were four months old. Packing for two young babies was a big challenge, and we had more luggage for that one night than we'd had holidaying as a couple in Australia a year before.' (*Sarah*)

One parent travelling with two babies can run into problems with the airlines, where restrictions on adult-to-baby ratios apply, usually dictated by the availability of oxygen masks. One major US carrier was faced with 'a very unique situation' when a mother booked to travel with her one-year-old conjoined twin girls, who are joined at the chest and share a heart. The airline's request that she pay for an extra seat to comply with safety regulations, as three oxygen masks would be required, was rejected by the angry mother, and the carrier subsequently let the infants travel free.

Opera singer Sinéad knows all about travelling, with and without her twins. Soon after she resumed work following their birth the telephone rang one evening at her Brussels home. 'We need you urgently. Can you be on the first plane tomorrow morning?' Taken by surprise, she enquired: 'Excuse me, where am I flying to?', before learning that she was to appear the following evening at the Vienna State Opera. In a whirlwind of babysitting arrangements and preparing bottles for the next day, she cast her eye over the score. There was no time for nerves. Her performance was a great success, and then it was back to the babies in Brussels. A couple of years later the twins themselves were three-year-old jet-setters. Early one morning a sleepy Emilie announced: 'I am so tired. I sleep in Berlin and Paris and New York and Brussels.'

'As the tyres hit the runway my two-year-old twin boys clapped and cheered loudly. We were the last to disembark, and as we shuffled up the aisle the cockpit door opened. Out stepped the captain. 'Would you boys like to come and see where we fly the plane?' Although passengers are barred from the flight deck, twin toddlers were clearly not viewed as a threat to national security! As the boys sat in the hot seats, eyeing up the plethora of plugs and switches, the captain reassured us. "They can touch anything they like." It turned out that he also had twins.' (*Susan*)

On location

Films and advertising provide an early career opportunity for some twins

'Why don't you try my twins? They're real pro's.' After a long day on the beach Julia had retired to the hotel bar, where she struck up a conversation with the woman standing next to her, a photographer who had flown out to the Spanish holiday resort for a photo shoot. Her assignment was for a high-class children's fashion magazine, and she was scouting for talent to model the latest in designer wear for youngsters.

Julia had arrived in Germany from her native Russia soon after the fall of the Berlin wall, at a time when travel restrictions from former eastern bloc countries were easing. She settled in Berlin, working as an airline stewardess and savouring the opportunity to escape from the cold north to warmer climes. Her good looks also enabled her to work on her days off from flying, playing minor roles in television and cinema films.

The news that they were expecting twin boys, later to prove to be identical, had come as a shock to Julia and partner Stefan, but she launched herself enthusiastically into the new role of mother to Vincent and Tizian. With her experience, she saw the potential for them to enjoy the benefits of part-time acting and modelling assignments, and she signed them up with an agency shortly after their third birthday.

Soon walk-on parts were rolling in. There were fun days out, as the boys dressed up in period costumes and then enjoyed watching themselves on the big screen at the end of the day. The pocket money was also handy for buying toys for the playroom and garden. By the age of five they had an impressive array of photos and mementoes on display in their home. They have done cameo assignments in full-length feature films, long-running soap operas and popular television series, on one occasion being filmed pretending to be ill on the children's ward. The boys act both together and alone, the work is fun and varied, and the looks on their faces leave little doubt that they love it.

The fashion photographer was delighted at the outcome of her casual conversation in the hotel bar. When Julia introduced her to

Tizian and Vincent she thought that their blond hair and finely chiselled Slav cheekbones were perfect for the assignment. Soon they were smiling at another job well done, another magazine to add to the collection, and another fee for toys back home. Everyone was happy.

Julia is not the only one to have seen the opportunity, and there are agencies specialising in twins of all ages for modelling work. She had seen little point in registering her boys earlier than three, as twin toddlers can be a handful at the best of times, and she felt that sitting still would have been too much to ask. Nevertheless there is a particular demand for identical-looking twins for filming when a baby or a toddler is required. Stringent controls on the periods for which such young children can work mean that identical twins can be used to double the effective shooting time on very expensive sets.

Sir! Sir! The bell's gone

School marks a new phase in the life of any child

Tina had spent the past four and a half years looking after her two little twin girls, with each day revolving around them from their birth until now. Occasionally she had been overwhelmed by having two babies to look after, and later by having two children of the same age to raise, with no previous experience to call upon. Now the girls were getting older, and Tina was confronting a major change in her own life. Their first day at school had left a gap in their mother's world. There was no younger child waiting at home, looking forward to extra time with mum, and no more childish bickering or frenetic tearing about the house. Instead silence awaited her. Or perhaps this was the peace and quiet she had so often yearned for during those long toddler days, but deep down never really wanted?

Sheila remembers the same experience, but a year later it was easier. 'On the first day back at school after the long summer break, my five-year-old twins, now in their second year of full-time education, were excited at the thought of seeing their friends again after six weeks. One year on from their first day at school, they were much more comfortable at being left. Sharing the same class meant that they could look to each other for mutual support.'

Sarah's identical twin girls have different birthdays, and different dates on their birth certificates. Lexus arrived at 11.20 p.m. on 31 August, but her sister Amber followed just after midnight, early in the morning of 1 September. An amusing oddity, but also a potential problem. In most of Britain the cut-off date for school-year admissions is 31 August, and according to the rules one of the twins will not start school until a year after the other. Sarah is determined that this will not happen, and she is negotiating with the local authority while they are still babies. 'There's no way you can have Amber sitting at home while Lexus goes to school. It would be desperately unfair on her to be excluded while her twin has all the fun.'

Although an extreme example, Sarah's case highlights a more common problem. Almost all parents would wish their twins to go to the same school, but circumstances do arise in which places are not available for both. The government has been sympathetic, and has issued 'advice' that school admission codes should in future ensure that multiple-birth children are not split up and placed in different schools against their parents' wishes. However local bureaucracy has not always been helpful, and problems are likely to continue to arise until the government converts advice into legislation.

Some parents of twins are also anxious that their children should be kept together in the same class, while others feel equally strongly that they should be separated. Providing such a choice presents obvious practical difficulties, in that many primary schools have only one class per year group, while as the children get older possible differences in educational attainment may also influence their placement. In general, teachers are now being asked to consult with parents about whether to allocate twins to the same or separate classes, although the decision remains with the school.

A pair? Or only brother and sister?

Twins are not always similar

The relationship between twins can be complicated and intense. Toddler rivalry may continue throughout childhood, or even beyond, or it may mature into a stronger bond than experienced by most non-twin siblings. This is frequently the case for identical twins, but as fraternal pairs grow up the emphasis often changes from being 'twins' to being 'just brothers or sisters'. Differences can become even more apparent when the two are of opposite sexes.

Alexander and Kate were born prematurely, like many twins, and they spent their first three weeks in hospital. Once home, they attracted the attention usual for newborn twins, and mother Charlotte comments that while they were babies her experience was similar to that reported by most other mothers of twins. But changes started to appear when they became toddlers and began to socialise with other children. Gradually they formed their individual friendships, with Kate tending to play with girls and Alexander with boys, and by the time they reached school age this had become an established pattern. There were, Charlotte recalls, a couple of 'family' friends, including another set of twins, but otherwise the children moved in largely separate circles.

Their primary school only had one class per year group, so that the question of putting them into the same or different classes did not arise, but at fourteen and in secondary school they are now separated. Other differences are emerging, as in recent exam results. Despite Kate's conscientious efforts her marks were far below Alexander's, who sailed through on the minimum of work. On the other hand Kate is clearly more mature and already rather grown-up compared to her brother.

Charlotte notes that even at fourteen the teenagers are both quite physical, and impromptu wrestling bouts still cause much mirth despite the frequent tears at the end. 'Deep down they adore each other – I hope – although they can also be unkind.' They still fight a lot, something which Charlotte attributes to them being the same age. Her brother's four children, all with age gaps of at least two years, never seem to tussle in quite the same way.

Within the family, Alexander and Kate are still known as 'the twins', but today this seems more of a statement of biological fact than an accurate reflection of their developing adult relationship.

'It's cool to be a twin!'

The transition to adulthood is also a time to reappraise relationships

Of American parentage, conceived near Chernobyl half a dozen years after the nuclear power station disaster, diagnosed as twins in Poland, born back in the States, and moved to Berlin at the age of five, twins Nick and Liz had an adventurous life behind them before they even reached school. They struggled at first, with a new culture, language and friends, but things became easier when they were accepted at the American school in Berlin. Here they flourished, speaking both English and German, and as fourteen-year-olds they had spent most of their lives in Germany.

The kitchen door opens, and Liz. comes in. She appears quite subdued, perhaps a little shy, yet she soon relaxes. After a brief introduction, the questions start.

Q: 'In order of importance, could you list the people you are closest to?'

Liz: 'Equal first are my parents. Then in second place my grandparents. Then in third place my cousins and my aunt. Yes, that's it, in order of importance to me.'

Q: 'What about the guy in the next room?'

(Nick has returned home from school and is playing music in the living room.)

Liz: 'Oh yeah, Nick, my twin. Equal first with my parents. I forgot about him!'

We all laugh. Then Nick appears, and he answers the same question without any hesitation.

Nick: 'In order of importance my Mom, Dad and sister are the closest to me. Then my grandparents, cousins and aunt.'

Q: 'What is it like being a twin?'

Liz: 'I like being a twin. It's great fun. I don't know any different. If my brother wasn't my twin, then things would be a lot different. As twins we share a special bond. The other kids at school moan about their brothers, but we get on pretty well. He can sometimes be a bit annoying though.'

Nick: 'It's cool to be a twin! People are interested when we say we're twins. There's a fascination with twins.'

Q: 'How do you manage with two cultures and languages?'

Liz: 'For us it is normal to be growing up as American kids in an American school. My English is better than my German. Occasionally I struggle with long German technical terms, which stack together like a string of Lego bricks. Next year all my classes will be in English.' (*She sounds relieved.*)

Nick: 'We've adapted well to life in Germany. Liz and I speak English together, unless we're at a party where everyone else is speaking German.'

Q: 'Are you in the same class?'

Liz: 'We're in different 'home room' classes. Some subjects we take together, but we sit next to our friends. We go back to the States every summer. There we have shared friends.'

Q: 'Do people guess that you're twins?'

Liz: 'Some people say we look alike, but they're always taken aback when we tell them we're twins. Last year there were more twins at school, and in one class there were two sets of twins and one set of triplets.'

Nick: 'The teachers at school are often surprised when we say we're twins. There aren't that many twins in school this year, which is surprising for such a large establishment.'

Q: 'Is it annoying sharing a birthday?'

Nick: 'We always have two lots of friends around. And a cake each!'

Liz: 'I don't mind having the same birthday so much, although it would be nice to enjoy my party without my brother's friends. Sometimes we get one present to share. Every once in a while we'll get twenty dollars for both of us. Generally though we get separate presents to reflect our tastes. As a child I would get a doll, and Nick a remote-controlled car. We'd both be happy with that.'

Q: 'How does it feel to have someone who's grown up with you at the same time?'

Liz: 'We'll have more to talk about and memories to share when we're older.'

Nick: 'The relationship we enjoy as twins is special.'

Q: 'What about children of your own one day?'

Liz: 'Having twins would be fun. Fun because this is one experience which only a few get to sample. Most people have just one child at a time. Twins are something special.'

Nick: 'I don't want to have twins of my own, but I would like more than one child. It would be important for the younger child to have someone to look up to. My Dad has always been my role model, and I have learnt a lot from him. I would like to have had an older brother and been led by good example.'

Nick has an interesting point. In families who have only multiples there are no older siblings to act as role models. Nick and Liz both agree that an older brother or sister would have been a positive influence, someone whose behaviour they could have emulated.

Kathie, their mother, stresses the importance of building up each child's confidence, cementing a firm foundation for their future and showing them where their strengths lie. She has helped her children to explore their own individuality, talents and gifts, exerting her positive influence since their early days. Even in their teens they continue to be affectionate towards each other, with no sign that they have drifted apart. 'My kids get on super well!'

Three of a kind

IVF has produced a large increase in multiple births over the last few decades

The triplets were the result of years of trying for an IVF baby, with treatment cycles fitted around Jemima and Andrew's international careers, working on projects in Argentina, Germany, Pakistan and Switzerland. They had decided on one last attempt just after Jemima's 35th birthday, and it was their sixth cycle. As this would be their last try they readily agreed to the unusual offer to implant three embryos, but they remained sceptical about the chances. At least, they felt, they would have tried everything before giving up.

Two weeks and a substantial bleed later, Jemima assumed that they had failed again, and she did not even bother with a pregnancy test. Although she started to feel sick, she put this down to her busy schedule and the stress of yet another unsuccessful treatment. But on her way to visit Andrew in Germany for the weekend, acting on an impulse, she bought a home pregnancy test kit at the airport. To her astonishment it produced a positive result. The IVF clinic scanned her soon afterwards and confirmed that she was expecting twins. In a week or two Jemima had got used to the idea, but the results of the thirteen-week scan sent her into shock. 'I don't want three! I'm not prepared! I can't cope!' She started to vomit, and the staff found her a bed, where she lay shaking.

At the clinic the prospective parents were offered a selective abortion to remove one, or even two, of the embryos, but they declined. At week 28 Jemima stopped working, although the triplets had remained a secret closely guarded from her perplexed colleagues, who asked as her bump grew: 'Are you sure it's not twins?' By week 34 Jemima was in hospital and being closely monitored, when concerns about one of the three little heartbeats led the doctors to advise an immediate Caesarean. Andrew made it to the hospital just in time to see Angela, weighing 2.0 kg (4 lb 6 oz), Sandra at 2.3 kg (5 lb 2 oz), and Samuel, a relatively hefty 2.6 kg (5lb 12 oz), enter the world one minute apart from each other.

Increasing the odds

Multiple pregnancies also carry increased risks of complications

After her first child, Silke had difficulty in becoming pregnant again, but after she was prescribed the ovary-stimulating medication Clomid she and her soldier husband Michael had a second boy. Anxious for a third child, and ideally a girl, Silke was again prescribed Clomid, and the desired pregnancy followed in due course. The early first scan was fine, but at ten weeks the doctor had startling news. 'You're winding me up! There aren't three babies? Triplets? Me?' He nodded his confirmation. As she left the surgery, grinning broadly at the fantastic news, she bumped into a friend. Her amazed response: 'I need a brandy!' Silke shared the sentiment, but with three little lives to take care of, she abstained.

At twenty weeks a detailed risk-assessment scan was carried out, and the couple were delighted to learn that at last they had a girl, or two to be precise, as well as another boy. The girls were most probably identical twins, and the doctor explained the risk of twin-to-twin transfusion which this involved. This is a serious condition where one baby effectively loses some of its blood to its twin. The girls' development would be monitored carefully to ensure that they were growing at the same rate, and not one to the detriment of the other.

At 28 weeks the pregnancy started to become difficult, and as is commonly the case with triplets Silke had to spend the rest of it in hospital. A Caesarean section was planned for week 35, but even that had eventually to be brought forward a few days. By the time she was wheeled into the crowded operating theatre an epidural anaesthetic had completely numbed her lower body. She was still wondering what was happening when she heard a soft noise, like a cat mewing. Unbeknown to her, the delivery was already well under way, and the cries came from her little boy, Jendrik, who weighed in at a 2.6 kg (5 lb 11 oz). Anneke, the second 'kitten', emerged one minute later without her mother even registering that she had been born, and was whisked away, pale and weighing just 1.5 kg (3 lb 5 oz). The fear that the girls had been affected by twin-to-twin transfusion was confirmed as identical twin sister Rieke was born, weighing a more robust 2.3 kg (5 lb). Her bright red colour was caused by the excess blood in her body, whereas Anneke needed an immediate transfusion.

Later, in the neonatal unit, tiny Anneke was the first baby Silke saw, and she was shocked. No bigger than a doll, her skin hung loosely round her tiny frame, and her eyes seemed too big for such a little face. Rieke, with her puffy face, red blotches and much larger size, bore no resemblance to her identical twin. Only Jendrik looked like a 'proper' baby, and he was thriving. Nevertheless they were all going to pull through, and for Silke this was a great moment to share and celebrate.

Touch and go

Risks present in a single pregnancy can be major threats with multiples

Daryl, a world-class rugby player who had taken part in many a fierce match with the New Zealand All Blacks, faced his toughest battle. He already had an eighteen-month-old toddler, sick and premature triplets had just been born, and the doctors had given his wife no more than an even chance of surviving the complications. With four very young children but no mother to care for them, he knew he would have to live up to the title of his team, the Glasgow Warriors, and fight on through.

Liana had been so excited at the prospect of triplets, but when she came round from the emergency Caesarean section she had no idea how serious the situation was. Her first waking thought was that all three babies were dead, but it was her own life which hung in the balance. Severe bleeding had been diagnosed as placenta abrupta, a condition potentially fatal to babies and in rare cases to the mother, in which the placenta separates from the uterus. The dangerous loss of blood had only been staunched by a full hysterectomy during the surgery.

Amazingly, the doctors had found all three babies hanging on to life by their tiny fingertips. They were whisked off to the neonatal intensive care unit, where Finn, at 1.7 kg (3 lb 12 oz), and sister Indy, slightly larger at 1.9 kg (4 lb 2 oz), required ventilation for four days. Tiny Oscar, only 1.0 kg (2 lb 2 oz), however, was a real fighter, and the only help he needed was a feeding tube through his nose into his stomach.

Happily the babies all survived, and so did Liana, recovering and returning home in time to greet the triplets when they were discharged a month after the birth. Daryl jokes that his wife is now more Scottish than Kiwi, due to the large quantity of blood she received in hospital. The average woman has around five litres of blood in her body, but Liana received a total of sixteen litres in transfusions.

Peas in a pod

Identical triplets are so rare that no one even knows the odds

After trying for some time for a baby, Lorenzo and Beatrice were delighted when the pregnancy test turned positive. They were still happy when a scan showed that it was twins. A few weeks later the news was more alarming. Triplets, and moreover identical triplets. Three babies, all the same. These occur in extremely rare cases, when the fertilised egg splits, and one part splits again. Beatrice wept tears of shock.

At the hospital the family received red-carpet treatment from the outset. The progress of the triplets was monitored by endless scans, most of them in high-tech three-dimensional colour. Beatrice was told that the pregnancy was extremely high risk, as the babies were in a single amniotic sac, receiving their life-giving nourishment from just one shared placenta. Potentially fatal twin-to-twin transfusion is also a risk for higher-order multiples. Nevertheless Beatrice enjoyed an active pregnancy, although her boss reluctantly sent her on maternity leave at ten weeks, to protect her from picking up infections at the clinic where she worked.

At week 31 she was admitted to hospital for observation, and six weeks before her due date, at week 34, she had a Caesarean section. She regrets not witnessing the birth of her boys, but damage to her spine from a previous car accident had made insertion of an epidural needle too risky, so she had a general anaesthetic. First out was Giovanni, at 1.9 kg (4 lb 3 oz), then Luca, at 2.0 kg (4 lb 6 oz), and finally Riccardo, another 2.0 kg baby (4lb 6 oz), each emerging at one-minute intervals. Riccardo was wedged into the bottom of Beatrice's rib cage, and he had to be tugged out, but he clearly had not been troubled by the lack of space. All three were able to breathe unassisted, and the only clinical intervention they required was a feeding tube, which is normal for healthy premature babies.

Early on Beatrice mastered the art of bottle-feeding all three at the same time, one in her arm, one resting on her thigh and one propped up on a cushion. She recalls seeing an exhausted mum who fed her triplets one at a time. No sooner had the last one been fed than it was time to start the cycle again. Lorenzo fed the babies at night, so Beatrice managed to get a reasonable ration of sleep, but the big breakthrough came at six months, when the babies started to sleep through the night.

A triplet buggy was out of the question, as it was too expensive. Instead the family opted for a double and a single pushchair, with Beatrice's Mum always helping on shopping trips. Ironically Beatrice has subsequently bought a triplet pushchair to help in her work as a child-minder, while Lorenzo is a waiter in a Berlin Italian restaurant.

Even the parents couldn't tell the triplets apart until they were two years old. At first the babies wore hospital armbands with their names on, until Beatrice crocheted some more stylish ones herself. Their Granny sees them every day yet still mixes them up.

In Germany children start school at six, and there is no school uniform. Since their first year the triplets have had their own sets of clothes to assist the teachers in the tricky job of working out who is who. At weekends they wear the same clothes, leaving passers-by to do a double take at the unusual sight of three boys who look exactly alike. To the boys themselves identical triplets are the norm.

Beatrice thinks it might be nice to have another baby, but Lorenzo is more cautious. As identical children are thought to occur by chance rather than to run in families, they should be no more likely to have a multiple pregnancy second time around than anyone else. Lightning never strikes twice. Or does it?

Three cheers for playtime!

Three small boys are more than a handful

Three is supposed to be an awkward number, ever prone to splitting into a pair and an odd one out. Technically, Ute and Oliver's triplets are just that, as Raphael and Sebastian are an identical pair, while Philipp is the fraternal member of the threesome. In practice the main problem with three is that it is a lot, when it comes to small boys. A certain primitive tribe's counting was reportedly limited to 'one - two - many', and Ute knows what they meant!

Playtime for twins is much more complicated than for a single toddler, and triplets add a further dimension. One child can have a little rocking horse, but with two the second one's fingers and toes are at immediate risk. Cupboards and drawers present the same threat, while an ordinary household door is a major hazard, threatening near-amputation of unsuspecting little sibling fingers in the jamb. Hence the astonished looks of 'ordinary' parents when they see the degree of child-proofing often required in homes with twins. Ute's answer was a specially adapted playroom for her toddler threesome, who were only allowed out into the hallway or beyond on special occasions. Visitors joked that it was like the zoo, with three marauding triplets peering out from behind the playpen bars which blocked their escape.

There were pluses and minuses. Ute noted enviously how single toddlers would spend long periods carefully constructing towers with building blocks. Out of the question for her boys. A brother would demolish any rudimentary structure before it reached the third brick level. On the other hand they were never short of playmates, and they happily shared a single ride-on toy car, perhaps because when one was riding the other two could play together while waiting for their turn. 'My boys would have fought to the death over one car', commented a mother of twins.

When they started at a nursery school the boys settled in quickly, although they tended to be a self-contained group, happy to play together while other children found it difficult to break in. Coincidentally or otherwise, two who did were my own twins, which is how we came to be invited round for tea.

Soon five small boys were rioting around Ute's living room, yelping with delight, banging on the windows and turning out all the toys. Then the 'That's mine!' game started, interestingly just among the triplets, although they were happy enough to share with their guests. Perhaps ownership is an assertion of individuality, particularly important among twins or triplets, who tend often to be treated as a group. Ute was used to the problem, and she had carefully written names on most of her children's possessions, so that disputes could be resolved relatively amicably. The triplets themselves wore neckerchiefs with their names printed on them, a handy aid for visitors and nursery group leaders, particularly as two of the three boys are identical.

It was a fun afternoon, but by the time it was over I was glad that I 'only' had twins, not triplets, let alone five!

Oh my quad!

If triplets are a surprise ....

During her first pregnancy Ann's bump was big and resulted in a large baby, so this time she thought nothing of the size of her belly. Ultrasound examinations in early pregnancy were not routine in the mid-1980s, so it was not until the midwife began to suspect twins that she was sent for a scan. Ann had started to come to terms with the idea by the time she went for the results the following week, so the doctor's words were all the more shocking. 'Congratulations, you're expecting triplets.' Ann had recently re-married and she had quickly become pregnant, without any medical assistance or infertility treatment. Triplets were a bolt from the blue. 'It can't happen to me', she kept repeating to herself.

The following months went to plan, although with the difficulties typical of a multiple pregnancy, and scans consistently showed three babies. Triplets rarely go to full term, so arrangements were made for an induced natural delivery some weeks ahead of the due date. All seemed to be going well, three babies had been safely born, and the placentas were about to follow. But as the consultant examined Ann there was another shock. 'I can feel something hard. I think it's a head.'

The extra delivery followed quickly, and indeed all four babies, two boys and two girls, were born within twenty minutes. Stacy weighed 2.0 kg (4 lb 8 oz), Ryan 2.1 kg (4 lb 9 oz), Lisa 2.1 kg (4 lb 10 oz) and Marc 2.3 kg (5 lb 2 oz). Ann had been carrying 8.5 kg (nearly 19 lb) of baby, each in their own sacs and with their own placenta. The surprise fourth baby, Lisa, had been crammed into a small gap between her brothers and sister, hidden from the ultrasound. Despite a poor initial prognosis she pulled through the traumatic first few days, although she still suffers from cerebral palsy and uses crutches to move about.

Ann's approach is pragmatic. 'It was a shock to the system, but it's part of everyday life, and you just get on with it.' Nevertheless she was relieved, when the time came, to find that daughter Stacy was expecting only a single baby.

Hit for six?

Four babies! It could have been worse

The sonographer took one look at the screen and then summoned colleagues. Soon they were crowding into the cubicle, peering intently at the picture. Not a word was uttered to the patient. Instead she was referred to the consultant. Jo was suspicious, but she remained calm until the doctor broke the news. 'There are definitely twins, but there might be up to six.'

It was the late 1980s, and Jo and Jeff had been trying for a baby for seven years. Eventually she was prescribed Clomid to stimulate her ovaries, but for a long time even that seemed to have achieved nothing. And now she faced the possibility of six babies. It was almost a relief when a follow-up scan reduced the number to five, and when at a later visit the number of embryos was confirmed to be four. Only quads! Fraternal siblings each in their own sac.

The doctor counselled them on reducing the number of embryos, explaining that this would lessen the health risk to mother and babies. Jo and Jeff had baulked at six, but now four sounded almost manageable. They refused. 'If something were to happen to the babies, then that's nature. If we're supposed to have four then so be it.' Jo's gynaecologist advised her to take it easy, and on no account to work. Yet she continued to slip away to her hairdressing salon, where she kept herself busy until she went in to hospital.

Jo and Jeff tentatively announced to friends that she was expecting twins, before finally admitting the truth. She is tall and slender, and her bump was tidy, confounding everyone's expectations. Her sister-in-law was pregnant at the same time, and one acquaintance assumed that it was she who was to have the quads. On her arrival at the maternity ward, Jo was confronted by a midwife ready to turn her away. They were expecting the mother of quads, not this neatly turned-out lady of modest pregnancy proportions.

The quads were born on the same day that another set of four turned eighteen, much to the delight of the local newspaper. Their mother rang Jo with a cheery but nonetheless realistic welcome to life with a foursome. 'All I can say is it's hell!'

Today Joshua, Ben and Zak are tall young men, and Joshua, the smallest baby, is an impressive 1.85 metres (6' 1"). All three study or work locally and live at home. Joshua and Zak are at the same university, while sister Charlotte has recently returned from a gap year spent travelling around Australia and New Zealand. They are easygoing and good company.

So what is it like being a quad? Ben explains. 'We don't know any different. People don't generally notice, as we all look different and have different personalities.' Indeed he becomes irritated when people expect them to be identical. People also tend to assume that quads are the same sex, and are surprised to learn that the three boys have a sister. At secondary school Ben and Zak were in the same class, and Jo recalls her surprise to discover at a parents' evening that the teacher had not realised that they were brothers. He was even more startled to learn that there were two more siblings. 'Quads, you know!'

8

The Quad Father

Living with four

From here to maternity

If twins are a shock ....

Andreas and Josephine already had two young children, but they wanted a third. Hormone injections were again required, but all went well, and when an early scan at four weeks showed two heartbeats they welcomed the news, as that would complete their family plans. Two weeks later there was another surprise. An empty sac seen at the first scan now also showed a heartbeat. Triplets!

For Andreas, triplets suggested Donald Duck and his identical nephews, Huey, Dewey and Louie, so his reaction was utter disbelief, concern and shock. The doctor tried to put the couple's minds at rest, explaining that real people do have triplets, and indeed her own trio were about to take their A-Levels. On reflection they felt encouraged, and they even started to look forward to the arrival of the three infants. They read that triplets are born on average at thirty-two weeks, and that the babies are generally healthy.

The eight-week scan was just a routine check on the babies' progress. Three-year-old Beatrice was excited about seeing a picture of her triplet baby siblings. As the ultrasound photo dropped off the printer she seized it enthusiastically and started to count the circles. 'One, two, three.' Meanwhile fifteen-month-old Katharina was scrambling around on the floor causing a commotion. Suddenly the doctor asked the nurse to take the toddlers out. As the door shut she broke the anxious silence. 'And this is the fourth child.'

Even today the shock remains with them. The tension is palpable as they recount the story. It was something which happened to others, not to people like them. They recalled news items of multiple births, but they had paid little attention. Now it would be their story splashed across the national headlines. Worse, they remembered from their earlier reading that the risk of disability increases hugely from a three to a four-baby pregnancy. On average, quads are born at just twenty-eight weeks, and each individual child has only a one in five chance of being completely healthy.

The doctors added that such a pregnancy was also a significant risk to the mother's health, and they recommended selective termination, reducing by one, or better by two babies. The couple refused. Josephine likens reduction to a game of roulette. There was no medical guarantee that the remaining children would be born fit and well, a healthy child might accidentally be destroyed, and the procedure itself might inadvertently terminate the whole pregnancy. She was quite clear that she could not kill a life established within her own body. Her faith and conscience would not allow it.

Josephine's gynaecologist, with her own triplet experience, was the most helpful. To give the babies the best chance of being born healthy it was necessary to sustain the pregnancy for as long as possible, and it was important that she spent the whole time lying down. With two toddlers about, this and the 'peaceful and harmonious environment' she recommended were not easy to arrange, but with the assistance of parents and a home help Josephine managed. Inevitably there were difficulties with her pregnancy, but she refused to go into hospital, even though this was common practice from the twenty-second week onwards with quads.

She was still pregnant and well at thirty-four weeks, but a Caesarean planned for a week later had to be brought forward when problems developed with the scar from her previous surgical delivery. Nevertheless she was able to go out with Andreas for a light Italian meal the night before, despite medical disapproval. As she arrived at the hospital she was excited at the thought of meeting her newborn quads, three girls and a boy. They all arrived within three minutes, each one shown briefly to Josephine before the midwives whisked them away to the waiting support team. Johanna was the lightest at 1.4 kg (3 lb 1 oz), whereas Alexander, Franziska and Charlotte each weighed in at around 1.9 kg (4 lb 3 oz), healthy weights for quads.

With hindsight, and in the light of the children's good progress, Andreas can now see the funny side of the step-by-step quadruplet diagnosis. He jokingly recalls that they didn't want any further scans, in case any more hidden babies came to light. Quads were quite enough, thank you.

Publicity and practicality

Cute quads in the limelight, but a complicated routine at home

Andreas was a pro at dealing with the press. His job as head of public relations at the German ministry for building and regional planning had given him plenty of experience. But he had not expected this. 50 reporters, each wanting an interview before they went to see the babies. He enquired which newspapers and television stations were represented, so that could he look out for their articles. 'All of them', came the reply. National and local, press and television.

The family were astonished by the level of interest their new arrivals generated. That evening Andreas and Josephine settled back to watch the national news on the television. To their amazement the quads were the second main item, following a report of a visit by Condoleezza Rice, the US Secretary of State. 'Pure diva!', Andreas jokes today, as he recalls how the family catapulted to overnight fame.

Later, after the babies were home, they grew accustomed to being referred to as 'the famous four' in their district, but this local interest soon subsided as the family became a familiar sight on the streets. However many tourists visit the nearby Babelsberg studios, where Marlene Dietrich made some of her well-known films, and which today is the Hollywood of Berlin. Camera-happy visitors were always eager to snap away at the unusual sight of baby quads, often without asking first. On some days the family had to push their way through a crowd on the pavement, with their two toddlers being jostled in the crush. Insensitive amateur photographers would even ask the two older sisters to move out of the way, so that they could take a picture just of the cute quads.

Even now that the foursome are past the toddler stage, the family continue to attract media attention, although they have turned down three separate offers for the making of television programmes about this phase of their life. Josephine feels that it is important to protect the children from unnecessary intrusion, particularly as programmes often focus on the stresses and strains rather than the more positive aspects of their development. However she and her husband were happy to be interviewed for this book, as they felt it would be a help to others facing a similar situation.

The babies returned home at the age of three weeks, and Andreas took a month's paternity leave.

Family life centred around eating. Milk for the quads, finger food for the toddlers, snatched meals for the adults. Against her better judgement, the professionals talked Josephine into providing her own milk, but in practice this meant expressing, using a double electric pump, and then feeding it to the babies from bottles. She laughs as she imitates the helicopter-like whirring noise of the machine.

When they left hospital the quads were on a four-hourly schedule, with Mum and Dad managing all six children unassisted. Andreas devised a hands-free routine for the babies. They were propped up by cushions, with the bottles resting on small pillows. Occasionally a baby would slip down, and all that was visible was the milk fast disappearing from the bottle. Andreas did the midnight and 4 a.m. feeds on his own, and he proudly notes that his all-time record was fifty-three minutes for feeding and changing the newborns, although an hour and a half was the norm. After washing up and sterilising the bottles, it was soon time for the next feed.

For sister Beatrice, approaching four, the babies were living dolls and she was delighted to help out, but poor Katharina, still under two, felt more deprived, as she couldn't understand why attention had been diverted from her.

Then disaster struck.

The limits of independence

With a sick mother, the family could no longer manage on their own

The strain of a quadruple pregnancy and providing milk for four babies caught up with Josephine. She developed mastitis, and she had to be admitted to hospital in extreme pain and with a dangerously high temperature after a bad reaction to antibiotics.

Fortunately Beatrice and Katharina had been visiting Granny, and they were able to stay on there for a time. Andreas had by now returned to work, but when he came home in the evenings he took over from the daytime child-minder they had engaged. He then had to do the night-time feeds on his own, and he soon realised that was not feasible for long. He couldn't do a demanding job by day and feed the quads by himself every night. He made an SOS call to the local authority, who promptly implemented a 24-hour roster of childcare to look after the babies.

The child-minder worked during the day, a twilight shift started at six in the evening, and night duty ran from midnight until eight in the morning. A record was kept for each baby. How much had been eaten? At what time? What was the state of the nappies? The house resembled the control room of a military operation, with systems to ensure that as the staff came and went on their shifts nothing was missed, and that each child was adequately cared for. This programme remained in force for the whole of the first year. The only privacy available to the parents was to retreat to the kitchen, as long as the nannies weren't preparing the next feed.

Such support was expensive, and the family budget was already strained by having so many mouths to feed. Fortunately the mayor of their city, Potsdam, became aware of their plight. He took it upon himself to act as a godfather to all four babies, and his office paid for the necessary childcare.

Next the doctors had to remove an abscess from Josephine's breast, but in her weakened condition she nearly died during this otherwise routine surgery. Her immune system had shut down, and after the operation she was quarantined in the intensive care unit to prevent her from coming into contact with any infections. She was no longer able to see her children, as the doctors feared that even a common cold might be too much for her body to withstand. Her mood was sombre, and she remembers mentally planning her own imminent funeral. Her mother was devastated. Josephine now laughs that it was the vision of endless bottles of milk and nappies which had terrified her, rather than the thought of losing her daughter!

After two weeks she had regained enough strength to be discharged, but the insecurity of losing their mother remained with the older children for a long time. They became agitated whenever a trip to Granny's was announced, as they associated this with having Mummy suddenly taken away.

Going potty!

Compared to a single baby, the nappies seem endless with twins, but ....

Luckily Pampers provided a sponsorship deal for the first eighteen months, but when the family had to buy nappies for the quads themselves they decided that it was the time to do their bit for the environment. The first batch of biodegradable maize-based nappies was not a success! They leaked and quickly produced unpleasant odours.

Andreas then calculated that with so many babies it must be worthwhile buying in bulk, so he ordered a full pallet from the wholesaler, plumping for a tried and tested brand. Josephine was astounded when an articulated lorry reversed into their quiet lane. The driver jumped into the back, reappearing with a forklift truck to deliver the 4000 nappies. It took Andreas two hours to unpack the shrink-wrapped nappy mountain and to store them in the cellar.

The first consignment lasted eight months, before the forklift truck re-appeared to leave another pallet outside the house, this time in the pouring rain. Unfortunately the outer plastic wrapping proved no more waterproof than had the maize-based nappies, so the outside packages of the new ones were wet. Attempts at drying them in the house proved futile, but they were not a dead loss. 400 were successfully re-deployed to absorb floodwater which had got into the cellar during the rain.

Potty training started just after their third birthday, as all four children declared in unison that they wanted to dispense with nappies. The frantic first few weeks of this daunting assignment were spent mopping up accidents.

Initial successes led to an unusual form of group learning. The children brought their little chairs into the 'wee room', vying for front-row seats whenever one of the siblings went to the toilet. The watchers then provided an animated running commentary as the live demonstration proceeded. The three girls were also fascinated by their brother's plumbing!

The next stage also has its hazards. On one outing Andreas was amused by the increasing incredulity of other users of the toilets as the six children emerged one by one from the same cubicle.

Child's play

Gradually the problems became less formidable. Now the children even have 'quad bikes'

As the foursome became mobile the house began to resemble a battlefield, with toddlers and toys strewn over every available space on the living room floor. Adults had to tread carefully to avoid stepping on one of the numerous children playing on the carpet. More space was essential, and a playroom annexe was completed in time for the quads' first birthday. This gave rise to more publicity, as the mayor and the local press photographer attended the 'official opening'.

The playroom had been made safe for young children, or so the parents thought. As an extra precaution the door handles had been fixed vertically, not horizontally, to prevent young hands stretching up, pulling down a handle, and opening the door. One day the quads managed to break out, bursting into a jubilant chorus of victory.

Andreas was intrigued. After rounding them up and herding them back, he waited and listened. Soon the door handle started to move again. He opened the door to discover the children working together as a team. They had stacked themselves into a pyramid. Alexander lay on his back at the base, and Charlotte and Franziska stood on his stomach. Then they heaved the much lighter Johanna up to reach the top of the door handle. Andreas was amazed at the toddlers' ingenuity.

As three-year-olds, the quartet are even more adept at combining their strength and determination in an effort to outmanoeuvre their parents. On shopping trips a favourite device is for the toddlers to exchange silent glances and nods before taking simultaneous flight, with Mum in hot pursuit. She has to be extra strict so that they know who is in charge. The parents are busy re-asserting their authority, which they feel was undermined in the early days by the succession of carers who looked after the children.

The local toddler group was another battleground for Josephine, with her battalion-sized brood. While the other mums chatted and enjoyed the social side among themselves, she was kept almost fully occupied darting around extricating one child after another from some minor scrape.

Going out with the family is much easier now than with the heavy quad buggy, which they adapted from a second-hand triplet model. Andreas and Josephine have treated the quads to four identical learner bikes for their popular outings. Each child takes the first one available, so that there are no arguments as to whose is which. The family are a sight to be seen as they cycle around the town, Mum and Dad, with six young children following, all on their bikes.

In fact many things are much easier now, even telling the children apart, as the quads are not identical. Their parents have focused on each child's individuality from the outset, and they have only dressed them in matching outfits on special occasions. Other people didn't find it so easy to distinguish them when they were smaller. Andreas recalls with a laugh that they had to take particular care at the christening. Each godfather held up a sign to make sure that the pastor bestowed the right names on the right child!

Double Firsts

Identical twins from Poland are studying the same subject at Oxford University

As the coach crosses the old stone bridge, sunlight streams on to Magdelen College's splendid sandstone façade, just opposite the leafy Botanical Gardens. In the heart of the city of 'dreaming spires' the banner across the newsagent's shop is sponsored by *New Scientist*, not by a tabloid newspaper. This is one of the world's most renowned seats of learning, Oxford University.

Bartek and Kuba are instantly recognisable, even in the crowded Queen's Lane Coffee House. These identical twins have the same tall, lean physique, blond hair and blue eyes, but they are wearing different glasses. 'We chose them so that people could tell us apart.' They have just returned from their 21st birthday party, back home in Poland's third largest city, Lodz. They had much more to celebrate than their coming of age, having recently achieved one of the highest academic accolades, a place to study at Oxford University. Not only that. They have secured admission to the same college, the prestigious 700-year-old St Edmund Hall, to study the same subject, Economics and Management.

They were born as healthy, full-term babies in 1988, just before the Communist regime collapsed in their country. They have spent their lives at each other's sides, so Oxford follows the pattern. In their school days they were in the same class, and their *Matura* (A-Level) results were uncannily similar. They took the same subjects, and their marks were never more than a few apart. In the Polish language exam they chose different essay topics, and the papers were externally marked by independent examiners unaware of their identities. Amazingly, each got 77 per cent. As on other occasions, friends joked that the stronger twin must have doubled for the weaker, but in fact both are equally gifted. Cheating has never been an option, not least because they have always taken the same papers at the same time but have been seated apart.

With so many shared interests, it was natural for them to follow the same course of study. Their parents are both doctors but their sights were firmly fixed on economics at Warsaw, Poland's leading centre for the subject. Yet they never forgot their teacher's advice to apply to study at Oxford, even as they embarked on a three-year course at Warsaw. Their exam results were excellent, and their parents encouraged them to follow up their Oxford dream.

In Oxford the colleges are the focal point of student life. The twins considered approaching separate colleges, but thought this was too risky, as one brother might be accepted and the other turned down. Instead they applied to the same one, hoping that the tutors would take their situation into account, admitting both or neither of them. What if their strategy had failed, and just one had been offered a place? 'We were optimistic', they reply, conceding that there was no fall-back plan. Instead they had early Christmas presents as they opened their letters accepting them at Oxford.

With just a couple of first-year students taking Economics and Management at their college, and under 80 in the whole university (out of 450 for all branches of economics), studying at Oxford is on a different scale from Warsaw, where the intake in their subject in the first year was nearly 1000. Recognising the need to learn for themselves, the twins have clearly defined boundaries. If they are preparing for the same tutorial they do not collude, and they only review each other's essays after they have been written.

They have grown up with the idea that people cannot tell one from the other. Kuba explains that when alone he automatically responds to his brother's name, and even their parents occasionally get mixed up if looking at them from behind. However their tutors don't confuse them, and people generally have less difficulty when they are side by side than when they are apart. They have slightly differently shaped faces, but otherwise there is little obvious to distinguish them. As youngsters a birthmark on Kuba's chest, now faded, made it easier for their parents to tell who was who. This was fortunate, as it took them a while to agree on names, so that they were known at first just by the positions of their cots, 'by the door' and 'by the wardrobe'! Their close family thinks the likeness is lessening as they grow older, although perhaps they have also become more adept at telling them apart. The twins affirm in unison: 'We're quite alike in looks and personalities.'

They live in the same college building, but on different floors, as they point out in an unconvincing assertion of independence. Even their sporting feats are similar, as both hope to gain the prestigious Half Blue by playing for Oxford against Cambridge at volleyball. Would their ideal partners be sisters, perhaps twins? Bartek dismisses the idea. 'That would be too much!'

Twins, or just born at the same time?

Most twins are non-identical, and their relationships may resemble those of other siblings

'That parrot's got to go!' The twins' mother was at the end of her tether. Just as the babies had been soothed to sleep, the parrot would start to bawl, skilfully mimicking the cries of the new arrivals. On good days the parents would rush to the nursery, only to be greeted by silence, with just the occasional sigh from the sleeping babies. On bad days the twins would wake up, and soon the air was filled with the efforts of three screaming pairs of lungs, competing for attention.

Kirsten and her non-identical twin sister Kerry are now in their mid-thirties, and they live with their own families in Britain. Yet Kirsten's accent immediately gives away her South African origin as she tells their story. The twins are the youngest of five girls, and their sisters are much older, 'more like aunts than siblings', with the age gap spanning seventeen years. Their mother only found out that she was carrying twins after she went into labour, so she decided to change the chosen name Karen into Kirsten and Kerry.

Kirsten recalls that some African traditions consider the first-born twin to be the junior sibling. 'I could relate to that, as I always felt like the younger sister, even though I came first and we were the same age.' As teenagers Kerry seemed to be mentally and physically two years ahead of Kirsten, causing the sparks to fly with their father by having boyfriends from an earlier age. Kirsten feels that 'we shouldn't be called twins, because we're not twins. We were just born at the same time.'

As children their relationship was fraught with difficulties, contrasting sharply with that of a pair of identical twins at their school. Kirsten thinks of them as the 'Vanessa twins', and she has to struggle to recall the name of Vanessa's twin sister, Jennie, as these girls seem to be etched into her memory as a single unit. That pair always played together and they developed at the same pace, compared to which Kirsten and Kerry were more like ordinary sisters than twins. Their relationship was tempestuous rather than harmonious, reflected in their frequent fights. Kirsten noted a similar contrast at university, where her fellow students included a non-identical boy twin who didn't get on with his brother, and an identical twin girl who phoned her sister without fail every day. 'It is so weird to think we're all twins but so different', she muses.

They have always been quite different. Kerry was more academic, eventually landing a responsible job at a bank, whereas Kirsten excelled at sports and became an artist, after first dabbling in music and drama. 'I loved the fact that I was able to say: 'I am a twin', but we never had the bond that you see with identical twins', she reflects. 'We were so different, but there must be some sort of link, as we had to grow up at the same time, in the same place, with the same friends. The irony is that we aren't alike, yet we do have so much in common.'

The bond between the twins has become stronger as they have grown older, and since moving away from their family and their native country. Despite their past differences they now enjoy a strong rapport. Kirsten always refers to Kerry as 'my twin', whereas the other women in the family are simply sisters.

Dead ringers

The organisers of Germany's largest twins' gathering are experts on life as a double act

'The dead body slipped out of our hands and crashed to the floor with an almighty thud.' Christian and Andreas giggle nervously as they recount tales from their German *Zivildienst*, the alternative to compulsory military service. Having declined active army duties, the identical twins were assigned to a civilian hospital, where they worked as porters. A corpse is literally a dead weight, requiring careful handling, and the twins had been instructed to move the body. As they manoeuvred it from the bed the trolley rolled away, and the body fell to the ground. They panicked, and ran to fetch help.

They are very matter-of-fact about their experiences in the hospital, and no doubt their stint has made them less squeamish about blood. Yet they managed to lose an amazing 30 kg (66 lb) each over the course of a year. 'We lost our appetite working there', Christian comments. Today these thirty-something-year-old men look fit and well, dressed in matching outfits. Christian leads the discussion, and Andreas laughs. 'If I start talking I'll never stop.' Their relationship works well, as they complement each other, and there are no interruptions or tense moments, just a smooth flow of conversation and laughter.

They have a fund of amusing stories of baffled patients who failed to understand why the 'same' porter had reappeared so soon after finishing his shift. Two ambulance men were always required to transport bed-ridden patients, and the supervisor, embarrassed by his inability to tell the twins apart, had a practical solution. Rather than working out who was who, he simply sent them on missions together. 'We were the *Doppelpack* (twin-pack)', they quip. The work at the hospital was varied and interesting, with each day bringing new assignments. Now they are employed by the same company, although in different departments, and the routine never changes. Their 'military' service was a refreshing interlude in their lives.

Christian and Andreas organise Germany's largest twins' convention, a mass day out which brings participants from all over the country to Berlin every summer. A recent occasion attracted over a hundred pairs of twins, most of them identical, who enjoyed a day at Berlin Zoo. What motivates them to organise this annual event? As children, they were frequently the centre of unwanted attention, whereas now they enjoy the limelight and giving press and television interviews. An additional benefit is that organised groups can often gain access to buildings not otherwise open to the public. Their trips have included a tour behind the scenes in Germany's parliament and a visit to television studios. These get-togethers also provide a good opportunity for meeting people, or perhaps even finding romance.

Their holidays are organised around twins' reunions, and they relish the opportunity to meet new faces and share in what they describe as 'family parties'. They have developed a system to tell their identical twin friends apart, including potential girlfriends. 'No two twins have the same head shape', they say. 'One head might be rounder and the other slightly longer. The difficult part is remembering which one is which.' Twins share a cramped space in the womb, and differing head shapes may be caused by pressure on tiny developing skulls. We put their theory to the test by reviewing photos on their mobile phones, and it seemed to hold good.

On the other hand they have not been attracted to the annual twins' convention in Twinsburg, Ohio. 'It's a bit too exaggerated.' This small American town throws open its doors each year to welcome twins, triplets and higher-order multiples to its festival. Since its modest start in 1976, with just 37 sets of twins, in some years it now has over 2000 families attending from all over the world. The highlight of the weekend is the 'Double Take Parade'!

Andreas and Christian are pragmatic about love, suggesting that an ideal solution would be twins, or two sisters who were very close and could appreciate the complex bond linking the men. Jealousy might be an issue for a girl who found herself sharing her boyfriend with his twin brother, in a non-romantic love triangle. Their current liaison was with a pair of twin sisters. 'The women usually decide who goes out with which twin. We go along with their decision.' They met them of course at a twins' convention.

Labour's double whammy

(*Conservative Party election slogan, 1992*)

The first twins to serve as British Members of Parliament, and as government ministers

'Angela Eagle', called the Speaker. A moment's awkward silence followed. Then: 'It's Maria actually.'

Maria and her twin sister are used to such confusion. For a time Maria served as a minister in the Labour government, sitting on the front bench in the Commons, while Angela sat on the back benches as an ordinary MP. Mix-ups were less frequent then. When her sister was promoted and joined the government too, so that they both sat on the front bench, there was no easy clue to help the unwary. Since the 2010 election both are on the opposition side, but the problem remains.

The Eagle sisters are the first set of twins to serve as MPs. Maria notes that the House of Commons library has unearthed other 'dynastic combinations', including mother and daughter, father and son (William Pitt the Elder and the Younger both became prime minister), and even two sisters. But no other twins.

The Speaker's is not the only parliamentary eagle eye to fail to distinguish the Eagle twins correctly. Angela once voted in support of a Private Member's motion which went against Labour government policy, but the tellers recorded the vote under her sister's name. This was embarrassing, as Maria was a member of the government and not allowed to vote against the 'party line', whereas Angela was at the time not so constrained. Maria's alibi was sound, as she had not even been present in the chamber, and the record was duly amended. They have also had problems with Hansard, the official record of all parliamentary debates, and the sisters have been forced to request amendments after the writer attributed comments to the wrong twin.

Their achievements are impressive. As ministers their working lives were split between their constituencies and their departments. Maria held two posts, as a parliamentary under-secretary in both the Ministry of Justice and the Equalities Office, while Angela was the exchequer secretary to the Treasury. Fortunately both prime ministers Maria served under could tell them apart. 'Tony never confused us', she says, recalling Tony Blair's talent for knowing who everybody was, and Gordon Brown likewise had no problem. Other colleagues, however, sometimes start a conversation clearly intended for the other sister. Maria has developed strategies to ease embarrassment, such as replying helpfully at a suitable opportunity: 'I'll let Angela know when I see her.' Even her constituents and local party members sometimes volunteer: 'I saw you on TV last night', without realising that their MP would not be discussing Treasury matters. Maria is clearly not bothered by these slips. 'It's part of being a twin. People think of us as "the Eagles". Sometimes I wish I had a pound for every time I have been mixed up with my sister.'

The twins are widely reported by the press as identical, but Maria contests this. Their mother was told by the doctors that they were fraternal, and this is the story the family is sticking to. When pushed, she admits: 'I don't know for sure.' The sisters do bear a strong resemblance to each other, and although Angela is left-handed, whereas Maria is right-handed, this does not rule out them being identical. They have not been genetically tested, so that the question has not been resolved. Their different hairstyles may simply be a conscious strategy, so that others can tell them apart.

There are more fundamental differences. Angela is the only openly lesbian MP, whereas Maria is heterosexual. When one political commentator described Maria as the 'heterosexual Member for Liverpool Garston' she challenged him. 'Why don't you say that everyone else is heterosexual as well?' Yet she can see the funny side. 'I am the only heterosexual MP who has had to declare the fact, as far as I know. When Angela came out, everybody reported that I was heterosexual. It's just one consequence of being a twin.'

The road to Westminster started long ago, but the sisters have travelled most of it together. Their mother suffered from bad morning sickness during the pregnancy, yet she didn't suspect twins to be the cause. She found out she was carrying two babies just one week before the confinement, and promptly fainted with shock. Angela was born first, beating Maria by just fifteen minutes. They laugh about it now, but birth order 'had an impact on the family psychologically'. As the older sister, Angela was automatically entitled to privileges, including the top bunk bed in their shared room. Maria was frustrated, branding such treatment as unfair, and it was not improved when, after younger brother

Andrew was born, she was subsequently labelled the 'middle child', just because she had arrived a few minutes after her sister.

The two women are highly proficient competition chess players. They played seriously from the ages of eight to eighteen, and were both ranked in the British top five girls, although Angela played more often for England than Maria. They were frequently pitted against each other, and they drew most of the time as they were so familiar with each other's game. If there was a winner, it would usually be Angela, which Maria jokingly puts down to her twin's more ruthless streak. Maria developed a strategy of detachment, reconciling herself to the idea of Angela assuming the lead. She says she never felt threatened when her sister was sitting opposite her, unlike some matches against outside opponents.

Their academic careers also ran a parallel course. They were the first in their family to go to university, securing places at Oxford, where they studied the same subject at the same time and even achieved the same degree result. Maria's tutor was the eminent Dr Zbigniew Pelczynski, no stranger to politicians, as he had previously taught the young Bill Clinton, later president of the United States. The girls decided not to apply for places at the same college, to avoid the risk that just one might be accepted 'at the expense of the other', but despite going to different colleges they ended up spending much of their spare time together. After Oxford Maria pursued a legal career as a solicitor, leading her ultimately to the Ministry of Justice.

Their father was an active trade-unionist, and both sisters joined the Labour Party in 1978. By 1992 Maria was the party's candidate for Liverpool Crosby, but the general election was won by the Conservatives under John Major. How did she feel about having unsuccessfully contested the seat? She quickly corrects me. She had pulled Labour out of a poor third to a strong second position, a great achievement, and she was proud to have been involved. Sister Angela successfully contested a marginal seat at the same election, defeating the Conservative incumbent, and Maria joined her at Westminster in 1997, when Labour swept to power under Tony Blair.

The sisters have shared many experiences, and have always had what Maria describes as an 'automatic best friend'. As children they were an emotionally self-sufficient unit. They didn't need to rely on their classmates for friendship, although I sense an unspoken regret that perhaps they missed out on one aspect of life in consequence. There has never been any major falling out, but they have both successfully established their own lives, although still within shouting distance of each other, even sharing the same personal assistant.

Maria explains that to most people being a twin equates to being the same, and this is why the press treats them as identical. People match them, like cards in a game of snap, and even assume that they share the same character. I had spoken to their personal assistant some weeks previously about meeting up. Perhaps her sister might also be interested in joining us? The response was clear. 'They're twins. They think in the same way.' Maria is keen to dispel this myth, insisting that she and her sister 'look and are different people'. True, they are the same age, they lived in the same room for the eighteen years to adulthood, and they have followed similar paths. People fail to see the differences when there are so many similarities. 'We're different people. We're very close.'

Life in triplicate

The long run

'As I was shaving this morning, I turned my head to the left and thought I was seeing Idwal in the mirror. As I turned to the right, I could clearly see Ivor.' Throughout his life Morgan has had to contend with other people's perception of him and his brothers as identical in appearance, and although he disputes this he accepts that there are strong similarities. When they reached 80 the press labelled them Britain's oldest triplets.

Back in 1928, long before ultrasound scans, mother Emmie already had three children, and she had felt the strain of this pregnancy more than the earlier ones, so that when Ivor joined first-born Idwal he was not entirely unexpected. The biggest surprise came twenty minutes later, as baby Morgan took to the world. Between them, the triplets weighed a total of 7.7 kilograms (17 lb), and Emmie had carried them to full term, unusually for triplets. Morgan describes himself as the runt of the litter at 1.6 kg (3.5 lb), but he soon caught his brothers up.

Their elder sister Gwenllian still fondly recalls the early days when she helped out with the newborn trio. Their arrival was perhaps most difficult for sister Betty, who was just twenty months old when the unexpected triplets turned up. As the youngest of the first three children, she had enjoyed plenty of attention from family and friends before being brusquely elbowed aside by her three little brothers. As Morgan puts it, in a rugby metaphor: 'We kicked her into touch, and just took over.' Emmie went on to have yet another boy six years later, and she lived a full life until the age of 93. 'She was rarely ill; she couldn't afford to be with so many children to take care of.' Morgan smiles as he recalls what a placid woman she was, and how she never raised her voice.

The family did not court publicity, yet the specially adapted pram would frequently be mobbed by well-wishers. Once Mum tried to wheel the new babies to visit her parents, a mile away from the family home in the heart of the Rhondda valley mining community, and the journey took three hours. Fortunately they lived just opposite the school, so they were later able to slip across the road without attracting too many inquisitive stares. As they grew older they went out of their way to avoid unwanted attention. Even today, at their regular lunch meetings, they endeavour to sit apart so that they are not immediately identified as identical-looking siblings. Morgan is quite clear that they are individual personalities, even if their physical looks are so similar.

The boys were generally known as the 'trips', as only their close family knew who was who. Yet to Morgan, his brothers are two quite different people, and he is one of the few who can tell them apart from behind. 'Idwal and Ivor are just brothers to me', he says, although he admits that the bond between the three of them is stronger than between the other siblings. He concedes that he and Ivor looked alike as children, and thinks that Idwal has grown more like them as they have got older. To the untrained eye, though, they all look alike. Even in their photos they appear to be identical, an impression accentuated by their mother's policy of dressing them the same. They never discussed with their family whether they were identical or not, and they have never been tested to establish whether they share the same DNA. Sister Betty says that they are not identical. 'She doesn't want any more accolades for us.'

Morgan passes over a photo of the three-year-old triplets in their class at school. A sign in Welsh reads *Ysgol Babanod Gelli 1931*, the Gelli Infants School 1931. Three little blond chaps are seated in the front row, wearing the same dungarees, and sporting the same cheeky smiles. Next he shows a photo of three attractive young men sitting on a motorbike, labelled 'The Rock 'n' Roll Years.' They all still have the same cheeky grin, this time with a twinkle in their eyes.

They grew up in difficult times. The Depression of the 1930s overshadowed their early years, and war broke out in Europe when they were eleven. As a bigger family they fared better than most. Rations for seven children and two adults were pooled to make reasonable family meals. Their father was a fitter, working in the mining industry, and the boys eventually followed him, Morgan working as a chemist at the mine, and Ivor and Idwal becoming mining surveyors. Call-up papers for National Service followed in 1948, but they were exempt, as mine work was classed as a reserved occupation, so they could continue their day-release studies at the local school of mines. Each brother attended his course on a different day, and the tutors often wondered why 'their' student was in college on the 'wrong' day.

The triplets all married within the space of one year, and the wives accepted that the brothers would continue to maintain their close relationship. One important misunderstanding was quickly cleared up after Idwal's future mother-in-law thought she had seen him taking another girl out. She had not previously known that he was one of an identical-looking threesome. The couples celebrated their golden weddings, although sadly Morgan's and Ivor's wives both died shortly after, following which they went on to live quietly on their own as widowers.

As children they argued a lot, but they respected their parents, who set strict rules for sharing. The boys had one bike, which they were each allowed to ride two days a week. Today the men still take turns, as every six weeks it falls to one of them to organise a lunch for themselves and their siblings. This was started by the triplets, as they felt the need for something regular to keep them in touch. Soon their other brothers and sisters were keen to join in, and now they are a family affair, enjoyed by all. Morgan confides that it is his turn next, and he has to find a location convenient for everyone.

The men live within 25 miles of each other, but Morgan feels that it is better for them not to live in the same town. If he goes to one of his brothers' towns he is often greeted by strangers, and it is easier to say a polite hello than to ignore them. Bemused that their friend was not with his wife, people on a nearby restaurant table mistook Morgan for Idwal on one occasion, and they were then surprised and amused to learn that Idwal is one of triplet brothers.

Perhaps the strangest coincidence was on a holiday on the Greek island of Rhodes. Morgan went to the same pub for an after-dinner drink each evening. Hearing a voice calling: 'Ivor, fancy seeing you here', he turned round to be greeted by a stranger. His brother used to sing in a Welsh male voice choir, and the man simply refused to believe that this wasn't his pal from back home. Even after explaining they were identical-looking triplets, Morgan could not shake his brother's friend off. 'He kept on pestering me, calling me Ivor, and it took me two weeks to get rid of him.'

Morgan was amused at the press interest in their eightieth birthday, and at the resulting tag as Britain's oldest surviving triplets. He was even more amused to learn that a close friend first realised that he was one of a threesome after picking up a British newspaper while holidaying in Spain. The brothers enjoy the friendship that comes from being triplets. There is a great sense of shared history, with over 240 years of common experience. Morgan has no concerns about the future and is busy planning a big party for their ninetieth. 'It's great having my brothers around', is a sentiment echoed by the trio.

Sadly, Morgan died shortly before the triplets' 82nd birthday, some months after giving this interview to the author.

The wall in our heads

(Saying in post-unification Germany after the actual Berlin Wall fell in 1989)

Twins divided for 30 years by the Cold War have found it difficult to re-establish their former rapport

'Mr. Gorbachev, tear down this wall!' Speaking in Berlin in 1987, US President Ronald Reagan challenged the Soviet Union to open up the borders from eastern bloc countries to the west. There was no response. Little more than two years later the citizens, first of Hungary and then of East Germany, took matters into their own hands. The so-called Iron Curtain was torn down, and the Berlin Wall was demolished and sold off in pieces as souvenirs for tourists.

Inge and Hilde were born in 1941, in the mountainous Erzgebirge region which borders onto the Czech Republic. There they were brought up surrounded by the traditional wood carvings of German Christmas-tree figures, a cottage industry which is a central part of the area's economy. The family was spared many of the hardships endured by city dwellers towards the end of the Second World War, and at a time when many of their fellow citizens were starving they never went hungry.

In an era before DNA testing, the girls were always considered identical, although as a child Inge was slightly shorter, so that even when she overtook her sister she was still referred to as 'the little one'. Today both have the same brown eyes, and their grey hair is similar. As children they were inseparable, and they would play tricks on unsuspecting acquaintances by swapping identities. Inge has fond reminiscences of her childhood. Of course there were arguments, but 'we came as a pair from the outset. We didn't know any different.'

When she was eighteen, Inge met and fell in love with Dieter during a family seaside holiday. She was still living in the Erzgebirge, while he came from East Berlin, both parts of communist-controlled East Germany. Yet like many young East Germans, they were attracted by life in the west, tantalisingly close in the other half of divided Berlin. In 1959 there was no wall, only a state frontier, across which people with the necessary permission could and did come and go, some on a daily basis to work in the west. Those without the relevant papers, however, could not, and any caught attempting to do so were liable to severe punishment as suspected defectors. Moreover those who succeeded could never come back, so that crossing to the west meant a permanent and total break with their families, including, in Inge's case, her twin sister.

Despite the potential complications, the couple went ahead and celebrated their engagement with their families. Secretly, they made their other plans. Inge remembers living in fear of arrest by the Stasi, the dreaded state security police, and she could not confide in even the closest members of her family for fear that she might be betrayed.

One day in 1959, on one of Dieter's visits to Inge in the Erzgebirge, the couple simply left her family home, without a word as to where they were going, and unable even to say their goodbyes in case someone suspected what they were doing. At the station they boarded a train for Berlin. During the journey the police hauled some of their fellow passengers off for questioning. It was an anxious moment, but Inge was travelling light to avoid suspicion. The address she gave in East Berlin was verified, and she was allowed to carry on. Dieter's relatives lived at this address, but the couple had no intention of going there. Instead they changed trains and continued their journey over the border into West Berlin.

Success, but at a price. Inge was unable to contact her parents or her dear twin sister. She had made her choice for Dieter and the west, but as a result her family had been sliced in two, and she might never see them again. She was homesick, but she knew there was no way back. 'We just had to get through it. Going back would have meant prison.'

While the privileged few could still cross from east to west and back again it was occasionally possible to get messages to Dieter's relatives in East Berlin, which they in turn relayed to Inge's family, to assure them that all was well. Then on 13 August 1961 rolls of barbed wire appeared in the streets of Berlin overnight. Inge recalls people jumping over the fence, fleeing to West Berlin, and at least one defector was shot dead as the borders were sealed. The notorious concrete wall was built over the following weeks.

As recently as June 1961 the East German government had refuted what they claimed to be western propaganda. 'Nobody intends to build a wall.' Now West Berliners felt cut off from the outside world, but no one foresaw this stand-off lasting for 28 years. Fortunately Inge found consolation in her fiancé, and in September 1961 they were married. It was a small ceremony, with just a few of Dieter's relatives from West Berlin, but Inge recalls it as a happy event despite the political turmoil surrounding their lives.

It was not until the late 1960s, after the birth of their first two children, that the East German regime briefly relaxed travel restrictions to allow relatives to visit from the west. For just one day at Christmas, West Berliners could apply for a permit to cross the border to East Berlin to meet up with relatives. Inge jumped at the chance to introduce her young family to their grandparents for the first time. And of course sister Hilde would also be there.

Their time together was brief, too brief to catch up on the intervening years with her twin, who was by then also married with two children. But there was more. 'The close bond which we had as children was no longer there. Since the wall went up, we had grown apart.' Previously they had been inseparable; now their lives were quite separate. Over the following years they saw each other infrequently, despite Hilde moving to East Berlin with her husband and family. Inge found crossing from West Berlin into the east too threatening. Border guards with large dogs at the railway station watched the crowd, machine guns at the ready, and each person was taken off into a small cabin to be interrogated by a team of officials.

Gradually the East German government made further concessions to visiting relatives from the west. In the 1970s and the 1980s Inge and her three children were able to visit her home town in the Erzgebirge. Sometimes her sister would be there, too, including the sad occasion of their mother's funeral in 1986. Although glad to see her family, Inge found these trips unpleasant. The East German border guards would treat them 'like criminals', systematically unpacking all their belongings, and even removing car seats to check for smuggled goods. Inge, herself a shopkeeper, now found her former homeland dreary, and the wide array of goods that she had become used to in the west just wasn't there. 'Either there was nothing in the shops, or there were lots of the same item, which everyone bought.' The roads were falling apart, and the houses seemed inadequately patched up. She knew she couldn't return there. 'Time had stood still since the 1950s.'

In November 1989 the Berlin wall fell, literally overnight, and East Germans were suddenly able to cross over into the west. Sister Hilde and her children came to visit Inge's West Berlin flat, and she again noticed how their differences had become greater over the time they had spent living apart. Years later, the gap remained. Inge was fully integrated into life in the west, whereas Hilde continued to hanker after many things she had known in the east. She enjoyed the newfound freedom to travel, yet like many others 'easterners' she remained sceptical of the benefits of the change. In the eastern bloc there had been full employment, and while women were expected to work they were allowed time off each day to do the shopping, as well as a regular 'household day', on which they could do the chores at home. For some, life had been easier. Even twenty years later Inge was still wary about broaching this subject with her sister, for fear of sparking off a heated debate.

The sisters still enjoy meeting up, and their children get on well, yet the families lead separate lives. 'Our relationship is not like it once was', says Inge. 'That's just how it goes.' Nevertheless they attended a recent Berlin twins' convention, happy to play the part again for the day. Inge is proud of their photo in the newspaper, surrounded by a sea of doubles, and both were looking forward to the next occasion.

Twins reunited

'Our separate upbringing had a much bigger impact on our lives than the fact that we're twins'

When Daniel, aged 25, had decided to try to find out more about the twin sister from whom he had been separated as a baby, he had not expected such quick success. A few hours after a holiday visit to the records department at the hospital where he had been born, he found himself standing on her adoptive mother's doorstep. 'What on earth do I say in a situation like this?', he asked himself. After a moment's hesitation, he knocked.

As a seven-year-old he had been asked to bring his birth certificate into school, where he noticed that his was different from the other children's, with the word 'adopted' clearly visible. His parents then revealed that he had a twin, assuring him that they would gladly have taken both babies, had his sister not been placed with another family just a few days before. Daniel grew up content to be an only child, and he gave little thought to contacting his biological parents until his teenage years. At that stage his awareness that he was adopted, and that he had a twin sister, increased to the extent that his mother tried to trace them. With hindsight he wonders if this was more to fob him off than a serious attempt to track them down. Perhaps she feared losing her son if he found his natural family.

Years later Daniel had to provide more documents in order to join the company pension scheme. For the first time he obtained his original birth certificate from his mother, which showed that he had been born in a town at the other end of the country. Holidaying nearby that summer, he set about sleuthing. Data protection restrictions are a more recent invention, so the clerk in the hospital's records department readily produced the information. 'Your sister's name is Pamela, and she was born on 29 March 1943.' As he was born on 27 March, Daniel was astonished to learn that his mother's prolonged labour had apparently resulted in a two-day gap between her babies. Then another clerk volunteered the name of his sister's adoptive mother, Mavis, and her address. 'I know her. She still lives there.'

Daniel's knock was answered by an elderly lady. Much to his

surprise Mavis was of Afro-Caribbean extraction. 'I'm Daniel, Pamela's brother!', he blurted out. He was even more startled to find that she had already guessed his identity. She explained that she had been a nurse working in the hospital when the twins were born, and she had remembered his striking red hair. 'Pam knows all about you. She's married and lives around the corner. I think she's away for the weekend but we'll go and see.'

Visibly flustered, Mavis took Daniel to her daughter's house, where she stepped inside the open door, calling out: 'Pam, you'll never guess who I've brought to see you.' The shock was too much for his sister, and she dissolved into tears before dashing upstairs to hide. Finally she emerged, and brother and sister spent the rest of the day together. On their way back from holiday Daniel and his wife stopped by again, this time for a planned reunion, before they returned home with 'some interesting news' to break to his adoptive parents.

As the twins spent time together on subsequent visits they became increasingly aware of their different upbringings. Mavis's father was from Jamaica, and he had studied law at Cambridge University before marrying the daughter of an English squire, while she herself was a Conservative supporter. Daniel, on the other hand, was a Labour man and a trades union member, so he soon realised that politics was a taboo subject. There were differences with his twin too. 'Apart from the fact that we were brother and sister, our separate backgrounds meant that we had little in common.' They were drawn together by the unusual circumstances of their reunion, but their varying outlooks created a potential barrier to their friendship. 'The saving grace was that we lived so far apart', Daniel comments. As they got to know each other better, they had fun identifying matching traits, including their reflective, easy-going personalities. Nevertheless Daniel maintains that their separate upbringing has been of much greater influence in shaping their lives than simply having the same parents.

Daniel's plan to introduce Pam to his recently widowed adoptive mother was not a success. Under stress from too many shocks, she lost her temper, complaining bitterly about her son having found his twin, and she let slip that there was another sister. Despite a later attempt, Daniel muses sadly that they were never reconciled. 'She couldn't forgive me for growing up.'

Many years later, by then in their forties and after both sets of adoptive parents had passed away, the twins decided to trace their family. The Public Records Office in London produced the certificate recording the death of their mother, Margaret, ten years earlier at the age of 60. Two years or so after the birth of the twins she had married a widower with three children, and they traced this family through the one who had registered her death. Later Margaret's sister-in-law, although guarded, confirmed that she had been aware of the twins, and she also dropped hints about who their father might have been, noting that there had been American GIs stationed in wartime England, and also Polish civilians living in the area. 'Just our luck. Our father was either Ronald Reagan or the pope!', Daniel irreverently jokes.

The search took them next to Margaret's sisters and their children, their own aunts and cousins. There Daniel and Pam saw photos of their mother for the first time, as well as of their grandparents, who were farm labourers. Then a picture was handed to them. 'This is Jane. She is your sister.'

Daniel had not forgotten this missing sister since his mother's hasty aside, but there had been no way of tracing her. Born in 1938, and almost certainly a half-sister by a different father, Jane had been brought up by Margaret's own parents to spare her the disgrace of raising an illegitimate child. As a five-year-old at the time, Jane would probably have remembered the twins being born. She had later married and left the district, but an aunt who was still in touch contacted her, asking if she would like to meet them. In the event she declined, and Daniel and Pam have never spoken to her. Contacts with their mother's other relatives also proved transitory, and ideas of arranging a family reunion in the local village hall were quietly shelved. Although it had been interesting to meet the people, and to fill in some of the gaps in their own background, the twins both agreed that the links were weak.

Nevertheless they returned to the search a few years later, this time trying to trace their father. Legislation in the 1970s gave adults who had been adopted as children the right to obtain information from the local authority and any adoption agency which had been involved. Unfortunately the county council's records yielded little, and the adoption agency had since been wound up, but they did discover that its papers had been transferred to a London borough council, where Pam's file was finally located. Daniel's own documents were never traced. 'I don't officially exist!', he quips.

After the obligatory counselling Pam was given access to her records, following which she laughingly rang her brother. Their mother had told the agency that the father had gone away, promising to get in touch with her, but she did not have his address! Needless to say he left before he could be held to account for the prospective twins. They had originally been placed for adoption as a pair, but were soon sent back. An apologetic letter from the family explained that they were being returned because they were 'somewhat scrawny' and would 'take too much raising', adding that the girl would probably be easy to place elsewhere, but 'the boy does not appear to be very intelligent'. A doctor had agreed that they were underweight, although pointing out that this is often the case for twin babies. However he challenged the statement about the boy's intelligence. 'I have carefully examined him, and he is perfectly normal for his class!'

The records did at least reveal their father's name, but a letter they sent out nationwide to those with similar names on the electoral register produced no results. On the off-chance during a visit to France, they even looked in the cemetery and archive at Bayeux, to see if he might have been among the soldiers killed during the latter stages of the war. They realise that their father is probably dead by now, and with no more leads the search for roots has reached its end.

Despite their unusual background and long separation, Daniel's relationship with his sister has developed over the years since they met. He smiles as he recalls how his then six-year-old daughter Harriet reacted to the news that her father had been adopted shortly after his birth. Some time later, she skipped up to him and asked: 'Daddy, what does it feel like to be adapted?!'

Postscript. During a 2007 House of Lords debate on the Human Fertility and Embryology Bill, a peer referred to an unreported court case in which a marriage between twins was annulled. They had been separately adopted as babies, neither was told that they had a twin, and when they met by chance they 'felt an inevitable attraction'. No further details have been revealed, but the peer quoted the case to indicate the need for children to have a clear right to know the identities of their biological parents.

Separated by murder

'People don't understand how great the bond between twins can be, not even other family members'

Nikki is remarkably composed as she talks about the death of her 21-year-old identical twin Jenna, although the wound is still fresh. 'I lost not only my sister and my best friend, but part of myself too.'

Their mother had been delighted to find that she was pregnant with twins, after trying for a family for ten long years and with several miscarriages adding to the heartache. When they finally arrived, she savoured every moment with her 'little miracles'.

There are many familiar twin stories from their childhood. At school the girls were obliged to wear name badges until the teachers could tell them apart. They grew up enjoying their close bond, sharing the same outside friends, the same interests and the same room at home. 'I realised that I was quite lucky, as we had the same memories, and there was always something to talk about.' There were downsides, such as the time when their parents were unable to afford both girls going on the same school trip abroad. At Christmas the children would open their matching presents in separate rooms, shouting to each other what they had received. Fun, but taking away some of the sparkle.

As young adults their friendship flourished, and they would often go away together, perhaps with boyfriends. Later, when they lived apart, Nikki would get into the car to visit Jenna every week, to catch up over a glass of wine or a film. If they hadn't called each other for a day or two, one would send a text asking the other: 'Isn't it about time you rang me?' Now there is no one to ring. Nikki sadly recalls the poignant moment when she had to stop herself from dialling her sister's number to share some news. 'Jenna's death left me feeling completely lost and empty, and the cruellest irony was that the one person I wanted to turn to is the one person who's not there any more.'

Nikki is sure that losing an identical twin must be worse than the death of an ordinary brother or sister, as they had done so many things together, from the day they started in the same class at school through to their shared adult experiences. As young children they were both dressed in the same outfits. 'If one of us spilled something we would both change into matching clean clothes.' As adults, the twins knew instinctively what the other was thinking.

Nikki had not been concerned about her sister's relationship with 50-year-old boyfriend Phil, because he had always been 'decent and nice'. But after a couple of years Jenna had begun to feel hemmed in, as he would turn up on her nights out with her friends, and what she had at first seen as his caring attitude changed into the feeling that he was controlling her. After ending the relationship Jenna started to date a boyfriend of her own age, but he called the romance off when he came to suspect that Phil was stalking them both.

No one knows the full story of that fateful June morning, or why Jenna decided to meet up again with Phil soon after her new boyfriend had walked out. All that can be said for certain is that after strangling Jenna in the car Phil calmly drove her body to a police station, where he confessed to his crime. Nikki still has nightmares, dreaming that she is in the same car while her sister struggles against her ex-boyfriend, but she is unable to move or to help fight him off.

On the morning of 24 June, Jenna left the family home and set off for work as usual. A few hours later Nikki's mother rang her to ask if she had heard from Jenna, as she had not arrived at work. Later in the day Nikki received a couple of text messages from friends, which she did not understand and assumed had been sent to the wrong number. 'I'm so sorry. You know where I am if you need me.' She later found out that the news of her sister's death had been leaked before the family were informed. Then came the phone call from the police saying that Phil had admitted to murdering someone, they had the body, and a police car was on its way to take her to the station. Nikki kept trying to ring her sister, but there was no reply. When she arrived at the police station the distraught looks on her parents' faces confirmed her worst fears.

Nikki panicked. She found herself unable to remember even what her twin sister had looked like, and the joint memories so fondly cherished were erased from her mind. She bottled up her emotions, afraid of the response which they might provoke in her already over-taxed parents, and bitterly aware that her identical looks would constantly remind them of her sister. 'At times I would be sitting on my own, wanting to go downstairs to be with them, but I felt that if I were there it would make it harder for everyone else.' Even today she struggles with the reactions of those nearest and dearest to her. 'People still call me by her name, and I know my Mum and Dad find it hard when I walk through the door. For a split second I know that they see her.'

Now the memories are returning, and she talks fondly of the times they shared together, but there is a great sense of loss. 'I feel like a part of me is missing.' Nikki's outlook on life has been tainted by this terrible event. 'Even after the first rawness faded, and when I'd find myself having fun and life seemed bearable again, those feelings would quickly turn to guilt. I still feel like I shouldn't have too much fun, as Jenna isn't here to laugh along with me.' Her anger towards her sister's murderer is understandable, but she is grateful that at least that he gave himself up to the police without the need for a search for the body. The family had to wait a month for it to be released by the police for the funeral, where Jenna's great popularity was evident from the large crowd of mourners.

The family's second ordeal was the trial six months later. Waiting outside the courtroom as the jury deliberated was 'the most intense thing I have ever done'. Nikki describes feeling as if her family had been on trial as the foreman delivered the unanimous guilty verdict. Not only were they in the public gallery of the courtroom, sat near the killer's relatives, but the case received intensive media coverage, leaving their privacy unprotected. Phil was sentenced to a minimum of 18 years' imprisonment, but Nikki and her parents share a concern for her safety when he is finally released. 'We dread the day when we might encounter him again. Being Jemma's identical twin makes the thought even more chilling.'

As a result of the stress their father was unable to work for several months, and he had initially to return part-time. Nikki herself had to take unpaid leave for three months while she started to come to terms with her loss. 'I try not to think about it too much. I like to keep busy when I'm on my own, otherwise I would be upset and need to take more time off work.' She has since changed jobs, partly to find a place where her colleagues are unaware of her past. Now she doesn't know how to respond when asked whether she has brothers or sisters. Should it be 'No', or 'I did have'?

Around her neck Nikki wears a pendant with a picture of Jenna and an image of a guardian angel, as a constant reminder of her sister. Although the girls disliked being called twins, they would affectionately refer to each other as 'Twinny', and Nikki chose this name for the floral tribute at her beloved sister's funeral. She struggled to cope on her first birthday without Jenna, particularly as the previous year had been a happy joint twenty-first celebration. The only other birthday they had spent apart was their nineteenth, and Nikki recalls fighting back the tears even then as her friends sang 'Happy Birthday' just to her. Now Jenna's absence is permanent, and Nikki took flowers and a card to her sister's grave. 'The cemetery is a difficult place to visit. I still feel like half of me died that day.'

11

Life in Tandem

Twins in the family

As they say ....

There is no point in going to bed early to save candles if the result is twins. (*Chinese proverb*)

'Where is the other baby?' (*Toddler twins visiting a family friend with a new baby*)

'Why aren't there two of me, like there are two of Edmund and Philip?' (*Playschool classmate of twins*)

'The smartly dressed lady at the hotel breakfast table next to mine had a three-year-old with her, and even the smooth cut of her tailored suit could not disguise the fact that she was also heavily pregnant. My toddler twins caught her eye, and she looked thoughtful for a moment, before murmuring to herself: "How efficient!"' (*Sasha*)

'Looking after my grandchildren, aged four and two, made me realise how hectic your life must be with twins.' (*Jenny to her brother, an older father with young twin boys*)

'The good thing about twins is that they're not triplets!' (*Father of lively young twins*)

'Why do those two girls look the same?' (*Five-year-old non-identical twin*)

'From the outset I have enjoyed the fact that the twins have always had each other. I am mindful of the rivalry between them but it has never been a real problem. They have a special situation, which will always be there, and they just have to learn to deal with it.' (*Katrin, mother of twin boys and a younger son*)

'As he elbowed his way to the front my six-year-old announced: "I'm the leader." His brother, used to his pushy twin, nevertheless staked his own claim. "But I'm the second boss!"' (*Sarah*)

'What do I do if I am naughty? Hide, run away, or blame my evil twin!' (*Slogan on a small boy's T-shirt*)

'Just you wait until they're swapping girlfriends!' *(Exasperated father of seven-year-old twin boys)*

'I have a twin brother, but I often forget that we are twins. To me he is just a brother.' (*Carol*)

'To the other half of me' (*Floral tribute from gangster Reggie Kray to identical twin Ronnie*)

Do they run in the family?

A dynasty of twins

The saga began in 1876 with the unexpected arrival of identical girls. Ernst's grandmother Emmy and her sister were the first twins in the family, so far as he knows. Later Emmy married an army officer, Ernst's grandfather, and unusually for those days she continued working after her marriage, although she gave up her post as a nursery nurse when she had children. Ernst's father was born first, followed by two siblings. Then came a surprise, as Emmy produced her own set of twins, a boy and a girl, born in the Friedenau district of Berlin, where Ernst still lives.

Twins were rarer in those days, and they attracted a great deal of attention. Ernst remembers that his aunt and uncle, who in their turn became respectively a nurse and an officer, remained close to each other throughout their lives. 'I have never seen such a loving, almost intimate relationship between twins. All five brothers and sisters got on well, but the twins were exceptionally close.' He recounts how the twins, by then elderly, went to visit relatives in communist East Germany. Accommodation was scarce, but even in their old age they were more than happy to share a single sofa bed.

Ernst himself belongs to the third generation of twins, born in 1943 with his non-identical brother Adalbert, and delivered at home by the doctor. There were five brothers and sisters, just as in their father's family. Ernst speculates that his mother Maria must have known that she was expecting twins, as she had tried self-consciously to cover up her outsize stomach when venturing out. Anticipating the additional workload, she had also wisely engaged a home-help.

Times were difficult. Germany was at war, and the family was living in a part which is today Poland. Soon their home was under threat as Russian troops advanced from the east. Grandmother Grete organised the evacuation of the whole village, finding horses to help the two hundred occupants to flee to relative safety. The twins were not yet two, and it was a long and arduous winter journey, but on the way Grete somehow managed to scrape together enough food for all the refugees. She later rejoined her own family in the East German state of Thuringia, after first ensuring that the villagers had been safely settled in Bavaria, part of the west. Ernst and his twin brother grew up in a village, and they were thus spared the worst of the terrible hunger which afflicted Germans living in the cities in the years following the end of the war.

Despite marked differences in appearance and personality, the boys were always referred to as 'the twins' at school. However at a fifty-year reunion in their childhood village, Ernst noted with interest that people now remembered them as brothers, not twins. They drifted apart after Adalbert's marriage, although since his wife's death they have become much closer again.

Ernst too has twins of his own. A second child was expected barely a year after the birth of his daughter Nina, but within the last few weeks it turned out to be twins. There was no ultrasound available in 1968, just a stethoscope to listen to the heartbeats. The doctor had to shut the window to listen very carefully to the palpitations before he could confirm the news. This was a shock so late in the pregnancy, and the first six years were very difficult, with no relatives nearby to help the family out.

In their early years only their mother and sister Nina could tell the identical twins, Ariana and Annabell, apart. Ernst himself had to think twice before putting a name to a face. Twins still attracted attention at that time, he notes. 'Even in the zoo they were more exotic than the animals!' The girls were inseparable at school, staying together right through, and even at forty they still go on joint holidays.

But they are not the youngest twins in the family. Ernst's oldest brother Siegfried has twin granddaughters, aged eleven. 'I really can't tell them apart, especially since they've stopped wearing glasses. They often wear similar clothes, and they have the same interests.'

Perhaps it is not surprising that Ernst is popular with children. For years he ran a photographic business in a friendly Berlin district, where he became a well-known figure in the community, nicknamed *Bilder Bär* (Picture Bear) because of his habit of stationing a wide variety of large teddy bears on chairs and parked cars outside his street-corner shop.

nvinced that the cries of one baby saved her twin

Our much-longed-for baby girls finally arrived at 33 weeks. Their birth weights were 1.9 kg (4lb 2oz) and 2.1 kg (4lb 11oz), and for premature babies they were in very good health. After a three-week hospital stay in order to establish breast-feeding, and to ensure that their initial hesitancy to breathe unaided was over, we were on our way home. We were over the moon, but it was also something of a shock, as we discovered just how much work the nurses had been doing at the hospital. We were very conscious that we had not one newborn baby but two, and that nature intended that they should still have been in my womb, but as the days went by we became more confident.

One afternoon, when the girls were still one week short of their original due date, I was at home alone with them. Maddy had woken fifteen minutes earlier than usual, so I took the opportunity to feed her quickly before her sister roused. As I settled into the comfortable couch, with one baby contentedly at my breast and the other blissfully asleep in her cot in the nursery, all was well. After many sleep-deprived nights I dozed off.

Suddenly I was woken by Saya screaming more loudly in the bedroom than I had previously heard in her six weeks of life. I started up, and looking down I saw that her twin sister had turned blue in my arms. She had stopped breathing. It was the most terrifying moment of my life. I tried to recall the CPR resuscitation lesson we had been given before leaving the hospital, but all I could remember was to put the baby on a hard surface rather than the soft carpet before beginning.

The coffee table was close by, and without a thought I swept the cups and plates to the floor. As the crockery crashed to the ground, I yelled my baby's name, desperate for signs of improvement. After I breathed some air through her mouth into her limp body, she coughed and spluttered, and began to regain some colour. The ambulance arrived, and took us all to the hospital in the small town in New Zealand where we lived. Later we were airlifted back to the larger hospital where the girls had been born, and we spent the next three weeks there. Both babies were closely monitored, and further episodes occurred. It was very frightening whenever they stopped breathing. Thankfully things settled down after a time, and we were able to take both of our babies home.

I dread to think what would have happened that day if my baby girl had not woken me up with her desperate screaming from the other room. Perhaps she had sensed that something was wrong with her twin? Our girls are nearly six now, and they are old enough to be told their 'special story'. One loves to hear that her sister 'stopped her from going to heaven', and the other one loves the fact that she looked after her twin.

More twintuition? Something similar happened in Lancashire in 2009, when fraternal twin Gemma hit the headlines after an apparent 'sixth sense' helped her to save her sister's life. Acting on an uneasy impulse, Gemma burst into the bathroom to find her fifteen-year-old twin Leanne in the bath, unconscious and under water. Had she not done so, her sister would almost certainly have drowned following a seizure.

It's grand to be a grandad

But parents of twins need more help than most

Just as the traffic was at its heaviest the mobile phone rang. Judith was driving, so John answered it. They didn't want to miss the call, as they knew that their daughter Rachel, newly pregnant with her second child, was going to the hospital that morning for a twelve-week scan. With a mischievous chuckle Rachel announced: 'They both look fine.' Then, after a pause: 'It's twins.' John nearly dropped the phone, then he relayed the news to his wife. 'It's twins!' Judith's eyes remained fixed on the road. 'Not another word until we reach the next motorway services', she said firmly.

Once they had recovered from the shock, John and Judith soon realised that their daughter and her husband Steve were going to need help. With a toddler and two new babies to care for there was going to be a lot of work, and a lot of potential pressure on the relationship. There and then they resolved to do their bit.

The grandparents moved in with the young family part-time during the first few weeks after the birth, taking over as much as possible of the night-time baby care. 'Once in the early hours of the morning the exhausted father came into our bedroom, holding a very unhappy baby', John remembers. 'When I asked him which one it was, he just shook his head wearily!' Later they stayed one night a week, to give the parents the opportunity to spend a few hours out of the house together, and to get some proper sleep knowing that the babies would be taken care of during the night. John notes with pride that he became a dab hand at bottle-feeding, and that he was far more involved in the child care than he had been with his own offspring.

Rachel is grateful. 'My parents made the first few weeks survivable', she says. 'Otherwise our lives would have become a domestic job-share.' But John is realistic about their involvement. 'We still have time to ourselves in our own home. The grandchildren are wonderful and have immeasurably enriched our lives, but care for them is non-stop for Rachel. She is quite amazing, the way she has coped with the pressures and so often come up smiling.'

Well-known twins

Some twins both achieve fame (or notoriety)

One of the earliest twin stories, that of Jacob and Esau, was recorded in Genesis, the first book of the Bible. After becoming pregnant, Rebecca, wife of the elderly patriarch Isaac, could not understand the jostling in her womb. Finally she gave birth, 'and behold there were twins'. Unfortunately they are also the first recorded example of twins falling out. With the help of his mother, Jacob managed to swindle Esau out of his birthright as the firstborn child. Not surprisingly, Esau hated Jacob, and the brothers were not reconciled until twenty years later.

Probably even earlier, in oral tradition, were the Greek god Apollo, patron of life, truth and the arts, and his twin sister Artemis, the chaste goddess of hunting, who were the children of the all-powerful god Zeus, the 'Father of Gods and Men'. Pollux and Castor were another set of twins in Greek mythology, but they had different fathers, a phenomenon described in Chapter 14 of this book and which was clearly known to the Greeks. Pollux, another son of Zeus, was immortal as a result, but Castor's father was human, so he himself was mortal and died in due course. In response to Pollux's plea not to be separated from his twin, Zeus placed them both in the heavens among the stars, where they form the astronomical constellation Gemini. Today they are probably better known as the astrological sign Gemini, familiar to all readers of horoscopes whose birthdays fall between 21 May and 20 June.

Interest in twins among the ancients extended to the Romans, who attributed the founding of their city to Romulus and Remus, supposedly abandoned as infants and brought up by a she-wolf, before growing up to fulfil their famous destiny.

Coming up to date (well, nearly!) and to the world of pop music, the 1960s and 1970s band the *Bee Gees* were a pair of fraternal twins, Robin and Maurice Gibbs, together with their brother Barry. They are rated as one of the best-selling musical acts of all time, with record sales thought to number over 200 million. The British boy band *Bros* of the late 1980s and early 1990s also featured twin singers Matt and Luke Goss, while still on the scene in Germany and internationally are identical twins Bill and Tom Kaulitz with their band *Tokio Hotel*. The principals of the Scottish band *The Proclaimers* are also identical twins, Charlie and Craig Reid, although *The Thompson Twins* famously were not. There were three of them, and they had very obviously different ethnic origins.

Sport too has its share of twins. Wilfred and Herbert Baddeley won the Wimbledon tennis doubles championship four times between 1891 and 1896, while Wilfred won the men's singles title three times. Fraternal twins Steve and Mark Waugh both played cricket for Australia between 1985 and 2004, Mark for over ten years and Steve for almost twenty. Steve was also captain for five years, and until his record was broken in 2010 he was the world's most capped Test cricketer. Brazilian identical twins Rafael and Fabio da Silva have been Manchester United footballers since their eighteenth birthday in 2008. Manager Alex Ferguson is alleged to tell them apart by the wedding ring on Fabio's finger, but the referee in charge of a League Cup match clearly did not have this information, as he gave Fabio a yellow card for a foul committed by Rafael. And in 2010 the Oxford Boat Race crew included American identical twins Tyler and Cameron Winkelvoss.

The cricketing identical twins Alec and Eric Bedser played for Surrey for over twenty years, up to 1960, Alec as a medium-fast bowler and Eric as an off-spinner. Alec also played in 31 Test matches for England and received a knighthood. It is reported that at the Oval in 1947 Alec bowled the first three balls of an over and Eric finished it off without the batsman noticing, although he remarked to the wicket-keeper: 'He's got a wonderful change of pace.' The brothers never married, and they lived together until Eric's death in 2006. Sir Alec described their relationship as 'a complete and absolute affinity'.

Identical twin brothers Norris and Ross McWhirter were noted for their amazing recall of facts, and they jointly founded and edited the *Guinness Book of Records*. Tragically Ross was assassinated by the IRA in 1975, after which Norris carried on alone as editor for some years.

The notorious 1960s London gangsters Ronnie and Reggie Kray were also identical twins.

Scott and Mark Kelly, born in the USA in 1964, are both NASA astronauts, and each has made several trips into space, although never on the same mission. They are the only twins (so far) both to have gone into orbit.

Jarosław Kaczyński was prime minister of Poland from July 2006 to November 2007, when his party lost an election. During this time he served under his identical twin Lech, who was president from 2005 until his death in April 2010. Lech and a number of other Polish leaders were killed in an aeroplane crash while travelling to a ceremony in memory of the infamous Second World War massacre at Katyn. Taking advantage of public sympathy, and playing down his right-wing views, Jarosław stood in the resulting presidential election, but although he was defeated his political career may not yet be at an end.

Unknown twins

Many well-known people have a twin

Elvis Presley, the 'King' of rock and roll, had a stillborn identical twin brother. The flamboyant pianist Liberace, reportedly one of the highest-paid entertainers in the world during the 1950s to 1970s, and Michael Jackson's brother Marlon also both had twin brothers who were stillborn or died at birth.

Other musicians with twins include Alanis Morissette, Jason Orange of *Take That*, Will Young, and Welsh soul singer Duffy.

From the stage and the catwalk, actors Joseph Fiennes (*Shakespeare in Love*), Scarlett Johansson, Kiefer Sutherland (son of Donald), and Ashton Kutcher (husband of Demi Moore), all have twins, as do models Jerry Hall and Gisele Bündchen.

Ghanaian diplomat Kofi Annan, United Nations Secretary-General from 1997 to 2006, had a twin sister Efua.

English heavyweight boxer Sir Henry Cooper had an identical twin George, until the latter's death in 2010.

Lillian Asplund, born in 1906, was the last American survivor of the 1912 *Titanic* disaster. She died in 2006, but her twin Carl, along with her father and another brother, perished when the ship went down.

Others are parents of twins

Both Britain and the United States have had a parent of twins at the helm. Like many mothers in earlier times, Margaret Thatcher was surprised by the arrival of a second baby during the delivery of what turned out to be twins Carol and Mark. President George W. Bush's fraternal twin daughters Barbara and Jenna also became well known during his time in the White House. And more than 2000 years ago another head of state, the well-known Queen

Cleopatra VII of Egypt, lover first of Julius Caesar and then of Mark Antony, also had twins.

Among sporting parents of twins are cyclist Lance Armstrong, winner of the *Tour de France* and survivor of cancer and persistent but unproven doping allegations, Swiss tennis star and Wimbledon winner Roger Federer, and former England football captain John Terry.

There are also many parents of twins in the world of showbiz and 'celebrities'. Elvis's only child Lisa Marie had fraternal twin daughters in 2008, and other actors with twins include Brad Pitt and Angelina Jolie, Julia Roberts, Geena Davis, Jennifer Lopez and Marc Anthony, Michael J. Fox, Al Pacino, and Denzel Washington. Singers Rick Parfitt (*Status Quo*), Julio Iglesias, Céline Dion, and P. Diddy also have twin children, as did Bing Crosby. So do writer Ben Elton, TV presenters Fern Britton, Gabby Logan, and chef Gordon Ramsay and his wife Tana. As noted in Chapter 3, actress Sarah Jessica Parker and singer Ricky Martin both have twins by surrogate mothers.

Last but not least, and the biggest showbiz name of them all, William Shakespeare had fraternal twins Judith and Hamnet, although the latter died at the age of eleven. Twins have long been a favourite device for dramatists, but perhaps Shakespeare's interest was more personal. Two of his plays revolve around the confusions caused by one or more pairs, *Twelfth Night* and *The Comedy of Errors*.

Twins galore

Over a hundred pairs, most of them identical, spent a day at Berlin Zoo

Outside the famous Elephant Gates, smack in the centre of the city, a harassed-looking young man was checking names on the list and handing out lapel badges. A moment later I saw him again on the far side of the crowd, hurrying-up the late-comers. Surprised, I looked back to the registration desk. He was still there. Of course! This was a twins' convention, and the organisers were themselves identical twins.

Berlin Zoo, one of Europe's oldest, claims to have the greatest variety of species of any zoo in the world, although after Allied bombing it ended the Second World War with just 91 animals. One of the city's main railway stations right next door is named after it, *Zoologischer Garten,* but is better known in the wider world as the *Zoo Station* of the rock band U2's 1991 hit album. Like so many attractions in this once divided city, the zoo has a twin, the 'Animal Park' in the former eastern sector.

The zoo is used to media attention. In 2004 two animal escapades hit the world press. First Bokito, a fully grown male gorilla, found a way out of his cage, causing visitors to scatter in all directions. After an afternoon stroll he was photographed sunning himself on a bench, before his outing was cut short by two zookeepers who marched him back to his quarters. Just a few weeks later Juan, the Andean spectacled bear, paddled across the moat around his enclosure on a makeshift raft, and after scaling a wall he headed for the playground, commandeering a bicycle on the way. A spokesman for the zoo later wryly remarked: 'Spectacled bears eat both vegetables and meat, but children tend not to be on their menu.' Nevertheless he was concerned to report that some fathers had been too busy filming the bear to round up their offspring.

The zoo's most famous twin is Knut, the polar bear cub abandoned by his mother and subsequently reared by his devoted keeper, although as his brother died at the age of four days he has since been a lone twin. Weighing in at only 0.9 kg (2 lb), the tiny ball of white fluff captured the hearts of the nation, generating a whirlwind of media interest, and the world's press followed his progress for many months. Interest faded as he grew into a rather grubby-looking adolescent bear, but on the day of the convention the press returned in force to view another photogenic spectacle, as over two hundred twins descended on the zoo.

The crowd milled around in front of the gates in a buzz of orderly disorder. Some were clearly old hands at these events, and were hailing their acquaintances. Perfectly normal, except that it was all in duplicate. Others were evidently first-timers, somewhat taken aback at finding themselves among so many twins, even though they themselves were twins. Most were identical, and dressed in identical outfits for the day. Casual passers-by and ordinary visitors to the zoo gaped in astonishment, apparently unable to believe their eyes. I was reminded of another Berlin event, the Wedding Dress Ball, at which couples dress up again in their wedding clothes. Confronted with a hundred brides outside the city's German Cathedral in the early evening sunshine, a tourist had enquired, 'Is it a mass wedding?' There appeared to be no such 'rational' explanation for all these *Doppelgänger* (doubles) outside the zoo.

The young man (or one of them) was standing on a ladder, shouting and waving his arms. Gradually it dawned on the crowd that he wanted them to assemble for the group photograph. The hangers-on, including mere parents like us, were shooed aside. Only twins were to be in the picture! My own little boys, among the youngest, were placed prominently in the front row, only slightly grudgingly, as they were clearly not identical, making them 'second-class citizens' in this assembly. More instructions were shouted. Poses were adjusted. Double smiles all round. Press cameras clicked. But what was my husband doing up that ladder? Oh yes, the hangers-on at least got to take their own amateur photos.

And then the gates opened and we all streamed in. Two by two, of course.

Second impressions

The humans went in two by two, Hurrah! Hurrah!

Perhaps inevitably, we were to be split into two groups. As we waited in the sunshine for our guides, there was a little more room to spread ourselves, and individuals – or at least individual pairs – started to stand out from the crowd.

Two sets of identical twins, one pair male, one pair female, were posing for a photo. 'Are you married?', came the question. 'Not yet!', boomed a friendly male voice, while one of the women giggled a reply: 'We only met at a twins' convention a few weeks back.' Nevertheless their arms wound around each other, and they were clearly hoping to add a touch of romance to the day. How convenient if both sets fell seriously for each other. No more worries about abandoning a twin as one sibling 'selfishly' tied the knot. And of course the new partners would know the intricacies involved in a twin relationship.

'We *are* married, and we are both identical twins.' A couple standing nearby briefly explained their complicated family. Husband Stefan's twin brother is also married to a twin, while wife Sandra is not only an identical twin herself, but also has identical twin half-sisters, fourteen years her junior.

Two attractive young men, Theo and Volker, were wearing the same outfits, sporting the same hairstyles and both walking with the assistance of crutches. They were entering into the spirit of the occasion, eagerly telling both old and new friends what a treat it was for them to be out just on crutches that day. Normally they use wheelchairs, as these identical twins both suffer from the same hereditary knee complaint.

Two more young men, two more identical sets of clothes, even similar names. Edgar and Edward were happily making new acquaintances and handing out their joint visiting card. This recorded their 'year of manufacture' and the fact that they are both computer specialists, together with their joint email address. They were, they added, shortly off to study at the same university. Twin girls Kathi and Gesa had travelled two hours from Dresden to Berlin, and these eighteen-year-olds obligingly spelled out each other's names, as though they were more important than their own.

Older generations were also well represented. Two attractive women, Annie and Diana, aged 48, were power-dressed for the day and attracting considerable attention. Both had followed the same career path as lawyers in Berlin. Their mother had also been an identical twin, and she and her sister had likewise shared a profession, in their case as doctors.

53-year-olds Marian and Mary were also dressed to kill. Despite their differing surnames – they clearly hadn't married a set of identical twins – they are very much in partnership. Their business card sports a stunning joint photo, and they are registered with a modelling agency which specialises in twins. Happy to be a double act, they are capitalising on their shared good looks, and like most participants at the convention, they didn't find my questioning intrusive, instead enjoying the attention.

By now a crowd had gathered, attracted by the unusual, sometimes even bizarre, sight of all these twins, many of them look-alikes in matching outfits. Most were adults, although there was a liberal sprinkling of children, and their ages ranged from three months to a mature 81. The adult twins were chattering together like exuberant teenagers on a school trip, but the organising young man (or one of them) still looked harassed. We should have been off by now. Hastily he herded the children and their hangers-on into one group, letting the rest choose whether to join or avoid them, and the two parties meandered away in the general direction of the animals. Glancing over to the big cats' enclosure, where twin lion cubs had been gambolling on a previous visit, I noticed that they had prudently decided to stay indoors today.

Private investigations

Doubles help with my inquiries

I had seen the animals many times before. So had my twins, and they were already bored with all the chatter. No cage full of owls was going to distract them! They wanted to go to the adventure playground. Fortunately my husband was also tired of being a hanger-on's hanger-on, and he was easily bribed by mention of the *Kaffee und Kuchen* stall opposite the playground (coffee and cakes, a German speciality). Now I could pursue my twins research unencumbered.

Acting as referee in a fight between her six-year-old identical girls Thea and Alexandra, Julia joked that at least today she wouldn't get strange looks from passers-by. She felt that she was among friends, explaining that she was rebuilding her life after a recent split from her husband. Life as a working single mother with young twins was difficult, and indeed only possible with her parents' help.

Two thirteen-year-olds pushing a double buggy caught my eye. Nicola and Julie, tall for their age, with shiny near-black hair and tanned skin, were going to be beauties. Klaus, their father, told me that their neighbourhood was dubbed 'Twinsville', with six sets of twins in one small street. The toddler twins belonged to one of their neighbours. Klaus recalled reading about a woman who had gone into early labour on a North Sea ferry, delivering her twins before the ship reached port. Their place of birth was recorded on the birth certificate just as 'on the ferry to...'. He had forgotten the place name, but it wasn't important. It was just another quirky twin tale.

Another group of twin children were busy throwing stale bread to appreciative warthogs, so I tagged on to a passing group of young adults. Nineteen-year-old Anke and Kristina are in their final year at school, where the teachers still confuse them. Identical sisters Lili and Isabel recalled another mix-up. 'How could she do that!', sniped one unsuspecting acquaintance, as he spotted his best mate's girlfriend out with another man. Only the night before they had all been together, enjoying an evening in the pub. Now she was walking down the street in broad daylight, arms entwined with another guy! But it was the other twin, of course.

At approaching seventy, Markus is still working as an electrician, enjoying an active life, and he is looking forward to celebrating their double 'big birthday' with brother Edgar in the autumn. He struggles to put into words how much his twin means to him. Despite going their separate ways after leaving school, their paths have always managed to cross, and they now meet up four or five times a week with their shared hobbies. Coincidentally they both married women called Angela, and they have even appeared in films together, as well as taking part in a university-based twins research programme.

'The nice thing about twins is that what one twin doesn't know, the other one does.' Katrin and Barbara are Berliners through and through, lively and direct to the point of appearing brusque to non-locals, yet with a glint of fun in their eyes. They had the bad luck to be born on Christmas Day, providing unimaginative relatives with an excuse for supplying just one gift to cover birthday and Christmas for both girls. Even their own children, so focused on Christmas, often forget their birthday. This year will be different, with family and friends joining in the double fiftieth celebration. With their colourful stories they clearly relish being identical twins, laughingly confiding that even their mother got the name wrong recently, when shown a picture of only one of them. As young children, having a twin sister helped their confidence. 'You always took a piece of your home away with you', they explained. On one school trip they crept into the same bed to comfort each other, while the other children had to deal with homesickness alone.

On any German outing lunch is not merely a matter of sustenance, but a central feature of the day. Happily we were approaching the zoo's central cafe, where we found the organising young man (or one of them), still harassed, remonstrating with the head waiter that not enough tables outdoors had been reserved for his party. Unperturbed, the man pointed out that the people occupying the places *were* from his party. Some, including my husband and twins, had got there early, and were already tucking into the sausages.

Redoubled efforts

Or twinned out?

The two parties, it appeared, were to swap over in the afternoon. But suddenly continuing to stroll and chat in the sunny outdoors seemed more attractive than a guided tour 'behind the scenes' among the cages. Moreover my husband, replete with coffee, cakes and sausages, was surprisingly unenthusiastic about a repeat visit to the playground. Switching groups would also enable me to meet more of the twins. As we prepared to move off we sidled unobtrusively from our party to the other, hoping to avoid the eagle eye of the harassed young man (or one of them).

For 50-year-old Simon and Jonas, being twins is the most significant part of their lives. They share a flat in the eastern part of Germany, where recession has hit hard, and after working alongside each other for years they have struggled with double redundancy. One of them (I am not sure which), remarked that to him being a twin is the norm. 'I've had my whole life to get used to it.' The second baby had taken their mother by surprise, since when they have always been together, and they give the impression that this is how they intend to live out their lives.

Jenny and Carol, tall, attractive women in their early forties, with blond curly hair, were wearing identical lemon-yellow shirts, but despite their similar features they were two quite different personalities. Since their first twins' convention many years ago they have been regulars at gatherings throughout Germany, taking a day off from their own families in order to catch up with each other and with long-standing friends. They explain that matching outfits are strictly reserved for special occasions. 'We still love each other's company, but we don't like to exaggerate being twins. Some go just a little bit too far.'

The press photographers had reappeared, and shutters were busily clicking. Eighteen-year-old Charlotte and Caroline unconvincingly claimed that Wilhelm and Richard, nineteen, 'are just good friends', having made the journey together from Hamburg for the weekend. Their photo was published in the papers the next day, along with the group picture, which was prominently and widely featured.

Katrin and Kerstin, 45, in matching outfits and make-up, were sitting with other identical twins. Being a pair was clearly important to them, and their parents had given them near-identical names. My own non-identical twins, they thought, must be 'more like brothers than twins'.

Mathilda and Andrea, 79, one of the oldest sets of twins at the convention, told me that there was a tradition of twins in their family. The newest additions, still on the way, would be Mathilda's identical great-grandsons. Even at their age passers-by still stare at them, whereas they see other twins as nothing special, just 'two people who look the same'. Even so, they agree that in a twins' gathering 'everyone feels part of a big family'.

Julian and Laurence had enjoyed their hearty lunch, and they commented that for them this was simply a fun day out with each other, a nice break in a great location. They both live in a small market town near Berlin, and are happily settled with their own families. They were New Year babies, so they share the champagne on 1 January each year, but they don't seem to find being twins the intense experience indicated by many of the others on that day.

Many pairs, many attitudes to their relationship, many reasons for coming. One thing is clear. Even as adults, and especially as such a large group, twins attract plenty of interest from onlookers. Some relished the attention, while others seemed to welcome a form of anonymity as, unusually, they were not the exceptions but part of a crowd of similar pairs. On their own they would have stood out, yet today people were noticing the group, and not the component parts.

As we left the zoo the harassed young man (or one of them) was standing by the gate. He looked relieved.

13

A Risky Business

When things go wrong with twin births

Physician, heal thyself

Prematurity is the most common problem with twins, as two doctors well knew

As an obstetrician, Louise was used to delivering babies.

She had found out very early that she was carrying twins. During a stint in the maternity ultrasound unit, in the seventh week of her pregnancy, her colleagues had offered to scan her, and she had cheerfully accepted. There were no twins in the family, so the news which they gave her was completely unexpected, and it was far from welcome. As a professional she was well aware of the greater health risks to mother and babies in twin pregnancies. Yet she soon recovered her composure, and the worries faded away.

Her husband James was even more disturbed, and his anxieties lingered on. He is a consultant neonatologist, concerned with treating premature and sick babies, and he was uncomfortably aware of the number of twins who came into his care. He knew the range of possible complications, and that cast a shadow over the prospect of becoming a father.

At 30 weeks Louise was whisked into hospital for an emergency Caesarean section. One of her twins was not growing, and the blood supply from the placenta to the baby was under threat. Her boss, the consultant obstetrician, was to perform the operation, something she had seen him do many times before. She knew that she was in good hands, and she had no concerns for herself. She had also seen him deliver many babies safely into the world. But what about hers? Suddenly she was no longer a doctor, just an expectant mother. The babies were all that mattered.

The operation went well, and the babies were born safely, but they were ten weeks premature. How would they fare? Joshua weighed just 1.2 kg (2 lb 10 oz), and Kate was slightly heavier at 1.5 kg (3 lb 5 oz). Most parents would be shocked by such small babies, but James was quite pleased. He had feared worse, often having to deal with babies weighing less than 1 kg (2 lb 3 oz).

During the twins' six week stay in the neonatal unit he struggled to cope with his dual role as father and doctor. Entrusting his newborn children to his colleagues was difficult for him. He had worked with them for a long time, and they jointly

160

had successful outcomes to many complicated cases to their credit, but this was not the same. The patients were now his own babies.

As an expert, James wanted to know all the test results, and to interpret them for himself, but the nurses refused to release the information, insisting that he discuss it with 'the doctors'. The stress of having two premature babies was compounded by the delicate professional situation. There was a fine line between asking for information and interfering, or even questioning a colleague's decisions. The reply was always the same: 'You are now a parent, not a doctor.' During the stress of an emergency delivery Louise had had no time to worry about any conflict between being a doctor and a mother, but during the long weeks while his twins were in the hospital James found it hard to be 'just a father'.

This story has a happy ending. Today Kate and Joshua are lively toddlers, running around the house, proudly wearing their wellington boots. 'They adore shoes', Louise says, 'and they love to show off any form of footwear to visitors.

When your twin can threaten your life

Identical twins face a unique risk in the womb

Wendy was delighted that her pregnancy had lasted until week 37, freeing her twins of the risks associated with prematurity. She beamed proudly as the midwife held up Calleb, a bonny pink baby, who tipped the scales at 3.6 kg (7lb 14 oz), but then the surgeon delivered the second baby, much smaller at 2.2 kg (4lb 14 oz). Moreover he was blue and in need of oxygen, but Wendy was relieved to hear little Joshua's cries, interpreting them as a good sign.

   Once out of the operating theatre she started to breast-feed her newborn babies, but the watching midwife was unhappy, and quickly called for a doctor. A couple of minutes later Wendy was left cradling just one baby, Calleb, and holding only a photo of her other son. Joshua had been hastily transferred to the neonatal intensive care unit. 'He was very poorly for the first 24 hours.'

Tests showed that the babies had suffered twin-to-twin transfusion, a condition specific to identical twins who share a single placenta, as approximately two-thirds of them do. Blood may be drained from one baby to the other through this shared placenta, affecting their relative growth rates and development, as well as being life-threatening in severe cases. This is what had happened to Wendy's twins, explaining Joshua's lower birth weight, his blue colour, and the problems he was now experiencing.

Wendy was overwhelmed. Her first child had arrived without any complications. Now she had twins as well, but one of them lay hooked up to monitors in an incubator. 'Joshua had so many holes he looked like a pincushion!', Wendy laughs now, trying to make light of the apprehension of those early days, when blood samples were taken every twenty minutes. He was also suffering from jaundice, which was treated by phototherapy, where coloured light is used to break down bilirubin, a yellowish bile pigment.

   Each day Wendy wheeled Calleb's cot to the neonatal unit, stationing him beside Joshua's incubator. The healthy full-term child became known as 'the lodger', out of place among the smaller babies in intensive care. As Joshua got stronger, she sometimes placed Calleb next to him in the incubator, 'so that the babies could be together again'. She was able to negotiate a room in the hospital for herself and Calleb, as she could not bear to leave Joshua behind after she herself had been discharged. A daily commute between home and hospital, two hours each way, was unthinkable following her Caesarean section.

Another happy ending. After ten days Joshua was ready to go home. Wendy's boys are now boisterous five-year-olds, as lively as any child in their class at school.

The worst of starts

Back in 1970, obstetric and neonatal care were not as advanced as today

The situation was critical. During the delivery of the first of her twins the midwife's stethoscope lost the sound of the heartbeat, and the child was stillborn. Dorothy turned to one side and caught sight of her little boy, pale and lifeless. She never saw him again, yet the image of her baby remains engraved on her mind. But the second one was still to come, and the contractions had stopped. A rush to the operating theatre. An anaesthetic. Four litres (seven pints) of blood. Regaining consciousness, Dorothy asked anxiously through the haze: 'Where are my babies?' The midwife took her gently by the hand. 'You've just got the one.' Still ill herself, she managed to see her little girl briefly the next day in the neonatal unit.

Baby Catherine had emerged from the delivery in a poor state, as she had also been close to death. In his struggle to descend, her twin brother had kicked her sideways. 'Between them they had used up all the oxygen.' Her scores were worryingly low on the Apgar scale, which measures the responses of newborn babies. The consultant gave Arthur his diagnosis, but it was to be kept from Dorothy for fear of causing a relapse in her own condition. Catherine was brain-damaged, suffering from cerebral palsy caused by oxygen deprivation during the traumatic delivery.

By the time of Dorothy's next opportunity to visit Catherine she was six days old, but the mother sensed that something was wrong. Her baby's tiny neck was floppy, and her head was tilted back. Even as a first-time mother she knew that this was not right, but she kept her concerns to herself. After six weeks Catherine was allowed home, where she fed well and thrived, but her head still had to be supported.

Dorothy confided her fears to her husband, but Arthur followed the consultant's advice, still anxious that she was not fit enough for the bad news. Some weeks later they went to the doctor together. There he told her plainly. 'You need to know that her brain was damaged. She will never walk, talk or be educable.' Reeling with shock, Dorothy protested. 'But she smiles at us! She's alert! She knows us!' The reply was an unconvinced 'Ah! Well!', before they were ushered out of the room.

The children's physiotherapist followed. 'I can help you with your little girl. I believe you.' She was a lifeline for the family, quickly realising that Catherine's problem was a motor and not a mental one. 'She is very bright', she added. With her constant support and monthly visits she helped Dorothy and Arthur to remain positive. As the months passed Catherine started to provide proof that the doctors were wrong. Unable to crawl, she could nevertheless stand and wheel her brick-laden trolley around, beaming with delight.

Dorothy and Arthur felt it important for Catherine to have a sibling, but they waited until she was three and less dependent before sister Claire's arrival. Despite assurances that there was no reason to expect a further problem, their anxiety was inevitable. A Caesarean section was planned, and to their great relief a healthy baby was quickly and easily delivered.

Today Catherine walks with an uneven gait and her speech is slurred, yet she has a responsible job, drives her own car, and is married to Kevin. She has decided against having children, as raising them would present its own difficulties. Instead she devotes her energies to being 'the best aunt in the world' to Claire's children. She is highly intelligent, with an amazing memory to complement her outgoing personality. Mercifully, the consultant's prophesy was way off the mark.

Living with disability

Having one disabled child is traumatic. Two could be devastating

Gaynor's worst fear was silently confirmed. The physiotherapist's meaningful glance was enough. Toddler Lili had cerebral palsy. She had received the same diagnosis for her non-identical twin sister Beckie soon after their first birthday. Now both children would need a lifetime of treatment and care.

The twins were born prematurely at week 29, and as a nursery nurse Gaynor had some professional insight into their progress. By the time Lili was sitting up, Beckie's body was rigid, and she could only lie down. The health visitor and a physiotherapist thought that the stiffness was a temporary problem resulting from Beckie's early arrival, but as she approached a year old Gaynor became convinced that there was something more fundamentally wrong. She asked for a referral to a paediatrician.

After examining Beckie, the doctor pronounced the dreaded words 'cerebral palsy', a condition more common among babies born prematurely or with a low birth weight than in full-size infants. Despite her grief for her child, Gaynor felt some relief that at last the underlying problem had been identified. 'This will make or break your relationship', the doctor added ominously. But Gaynor and Greg had survived the first year with twins. Surely they would come through this, she thought.

'It was very frightening to be a new 'disabled' mum. Disability suddenly becomes your world.' Gaynor's priority was helping Beckie, who started physiotherapy and joined a special playgroup. Confronted by so many disabled children, many of whom were more severely affected than Beckie, Gaynor felt out of her depth. Yet the mothers had a reassuring realism about the struggle they all faced in their daily lives, and they welcomed her into their support network. Laughter was the most vital weapon in their armoury. 'You have to have a sense of humour about yourself and your kids. Otherwise you'd be overwhelmed.'

Lili joined the playgroup with her sister, but although the girls were progressing at different paces Gaynor began to wonder about her. She was romping through her developmental phases compared to Beckie and the other playgroup children, but when she was with children outside, Gaynor suspected that she was lagging behind.

The second cerebral palsy diagnosis came shortly before the twins' second birthday. The news hit Gaynor hard, and her tears were more for herself than for her child. 'I can't do this a second time.' Despite an initial 'mild' assessment Lili still faced a battery of consultations to evaluate and treat the condition. Their lives turned into a continuous round of medical appointments. Gaynor was caught by a speed camera three times in a fortnight, not intentionally speeding but simply overtaken by the events in her life. She was forced to slow down her thinking and her driving. The family could not cope if she lost her licence.

From the outset Gaynor learned the significance of 'tough love'. At Beckie's first physiotherapy session her instinct was to intervene and take the screaming toddler away. The expert's words were harsh but to the point. 'If you can't bear to watch, then leave the room. This isn't about you, it's about your daughter.' Physiotherapy is crucial for victims of cerebral palsy, as it keeps them supple and helps to prevent their bodies from becoming contorted, as was often the case in earlier generations.

Five years later, Gaynor's second pregnancy was accompanied by wildly fluctuating emotions, veering from sheer terror to absolute delight. The birth of a healthy singleton was totally different from the twins' traumatic premature arrival. There was no prospect of losing him, and she developed an immediate bond, proudly announcing: 'This is my baby.' Henry is now a lively little boy. Hurtling around the house, he brings home to Gaynor how challenging her role had been when the girls were young. Her son can play independently, unlike his sisters who needed constant supervision, and as babies couldn't even grasp toys without help.

The ten-year-old twins are delightful children, but treatment continues to be a major part of their lives. Lili's disability is relatively mild, whereas Beckie is more severely afflicted and requires a wheelchair. She has to sleep in gators, not dissimilar to old-fashioned leg-irons, and Gaynor has to massage her muscles during the night if she is attacked by cramp. The child is frequently in plaster, often following painful operations on her legs.

The strain has taken its toll on the family. The doctor's words years ago have come back to haunt the couple, as they deliberate over whether to stay together, or to separate, with Gaynor taking sole charge of the children. Either way, there are no easy options.

Pluck from the memory a rooted sorrow

(Shakespeare, *Macbeth*)

More than fifty years on, the death of premature twins is still fresh

'What lovely twins!' The elderly lady turned to me as we washed our hands side by side. Wisps of silvery hair framed a kind face, her eyes twinkled behind her glasses, and a smile played around her lips. It was a beautiful Berlin summer evening, and we were making the most of it. The balmy weather and the light nights were ideal for outdoor dining, with the fragrance of summer roses hanging heavy in the air. Impressed that she had picked out my non-identical twin boys from the array of rioting children in the restaurant's garden, I thanked her for the compliment.

'I had twins too, but I lost them', she continued. Caught unprepared, I didn't know what to say. A feeble 'I'm so sorry' was all I could muster, but I wanted to know more. 'My name is Hildegard. Why don't you come and sit with us?', invited the lively 77-year-old. We went back to the restaurant's garden tables, where her husband Günter, a young-looking 81, greeted me with an air of faint suspicion as I sat down. As the introductions were made he protested mildly: 'It was such a long time ago', but it was too late. Hildegard had already started to recount their tale.

She explained how excited they had both been when she became pregnant at 23, and how they had eagerly awaited the arrival of their child. Soon her bump was larger than expected, but they assured the midwife that they were certain of the relevant dates. It was 1954, and there was no ultrasound, so no more could be done. Contractions started during her seventh month, and Hildegard was admitted to hospital, where she progressed swiftly to full labour. A midwife delivered a beautiful boy, but suddenly a second tiny life arrived, unannounced. They were the parents of twin boys, small but apparently healthy. The proud father registered both births.

Then tragedy struck. Hildegard paused and took a deep breath before continuing. Baby Klaus fought a brave battle, but passed away just one day later. After their first-born had been taken so suddenly, they pinned their hopes on his little brother. Then tiny

Thomas took an unexpected turn for the worse. To his parents' utter despair, he died two days later.

Hildegard and Günter were devastated. They had experienced so many fluctuating emotions in such a short space of time, but this was heartache beyond anything they had ever known. There were so many regrets. There had been no time to get to know the twins, and they did not even have a photo. Hildegard did not dwell on the details, but her pain was almost tangible despite the passing of over half a century. She remained in hospital, where she was visited by the chaplain, dressed in his black cassock. She was physically healthy, but in her state of mind his dark outfit seemed ominous, and she thought he had come to administer the last rites to her. Instead he simply took her hand and whispered: 'I just want to comfort you.'

Günter comments that the twins had not survived because they had been too small and weak. 'We left hospital alone, with empty arms and hearts.' Today a more specific cause of death would be recorded, but of course the twins might well have lived had today's high-tech standards of neonatal care been available, rather than just a 1950s heated cot. Prematurity was often a fatal curse in those days, as it still is in many less developed parts of the world.

Hildegard and Günter allowed themselves some time before trying again for children. Andreas, a third son, came along three years later. For Hildegard, the new baby was some consolation for her loss, although she could never forget her first two. Even today, twins never escape her watchful eye, but her delight at seeing two children playing together is tinged with sadness, as she is reminded of her own grief. She and her husband have moved on, and they have made peace with their past, but they will always feel the gap in the lives left by the deaths of Klaus and Thomas.

Orphaned at birth

New technology, new risks. Older mothers are themselves vulnerable

'I have some bad news. Eva is dead.' Frauke put the phone down and stared into space, wiping tears of shock and disbelief from her eyes, as she wondered what would happen to Eva's two-day-old twins. She had been busily decorating her friend's flat, ready to greet the two new arrivals. As an architect and interior designer she had selected the nursery colours with enthusiasm and professional acumen. Now what?

As she approached her fiftieth birthday, with a miscarriage and various disappointments in love behind her, divorcee Eva's chances of having children seemed to have gone. Nevertheless she was not one to give up easily, and she was always ready to contemplate the unconventional. Eventually she persuaded her ex-husband, still a good friend, to supply his sperm for IVF treatment. Her part of the bargain would be to raise the baby single-handedly. At last she realised her ambition of a sustainable pregnancy, and she was delighted rather than daunted when it turned out to be twins. Frauke was more concerned. At 51 perhaps even the vivacious Eva had overestimated her strength. But she kept her thoughts to herself.

Eva was not taking any chances with the babies. With time and money to spare she left her native Berlin and flew to Florida for the confinement, as she considered health care in the USA to be superior to that in Germany. Two young women accompanied her as nannies for the prospective twins. Finally the big day came, and a healthy boy and girl were born by Caesarean section.

Two days after the operation Eva suffered a pulmonary embolism, a blood clot in her lungs, which led to the new mother's death. The combination of her age, a twin pregnancy, and the aftermath of the Caesarean surgery was too much. The new-born babies were orphans, twins who would never know the mother who had wanted them so desperately.

They were not abandoned, as their biological father quickly stepped into the breach, sweeping the tiny babies up in his arms and taking them back to Europe. They are now happy, well-adjusted children, thriving in the home they share with their father and stepmother. But as the twins grow up they are bound to wonder about the mother whose desire for them cost her own life.

Five years on Frauke still cannot disguise her sadness, as tears fill her eyes and her voice wavers. Yet there is also anger, as she voices her doubts about whether IVF should have been offered to Eva at the age of fifty, particularly on a technical basis which involved the additional risk of twins. Eva and her boys never saw the flat that she had decorated for them.

What and Why and When
And How and Where and Who
(*Rudyard Kipling*)

The trouble doubles?

They may not be lies or damned lies (as Victorian prime minister Disraeli said), but the statistics about twins are certainly confusing, while even the apparently simple fact of what *is* a twin is not always as straightforward as it seems.

One statistic stands out. There are a lot more twins than there used to be, something apparent even to the casual observer, as there are twice as many double buggies on the High Street than there were thirty years ago. After that it gets complicated. The total number of babies born fluctuates unpredictably from year to year, as well as changing significantly over longer periods, and the number of twins varies with the total. The development of IVF, or in-vitro fertilisation, has made important differences since the world's first 'test-tube baby' was born in England in 1978, as IVF produces a far higher proportion of twins. To further confuse the picture there is a clear, although so far not well understood, increase in the frequency of twins even in natural pregnancies.

In recent decades the number of maternities (single births, twins and multiples) in the UK has been rising, and in 2008 it was 20 per cent higher than in 1977, but over the same period the number of twins increased by 90 per cent. Hence 5700 more pairs were born in 2008 than in 1977 (12,000 compared to 6300), whereas only 1200 more would have been expected from the increase in the total number of maternities alone. IVF was responsible for rather over half of the extra 4500 pairs of twins, some 2500, while the balance of 2000 was due to a higher twinning rate in natural pregnancies.

In 1977 one UK maternity in 104 produced twins, the then natural twinning rate, although this had probably already been increased by the fertility drugs which preceded IVF. In 2008 one in 82 mothers gave birth to naturally conceived twins, a significant increase of 27 per cent. In sharp contrast, twins resulted from almost one in four IVF maternities. Nevertheless, and despite a growing link in the public mind between twins and IVF, most twins – almost 80 per cent – were still naturally conceived.

Moreover the number of pairs of twins born, together with the much smaller number of triplets and higher-order multiples, remained small as a proportion of all maternities, only 1½ per cent in 2008. There were, of course, twice as many individual twin babies, 24,000 or 3 per cent of the total of 794,000 born in that year.

Helping the stork

Another incompletely understood trend in recent decades has been a decline in human fertility in developed countries, leading to a considerable rise in the number of childless couples seeking help. Techniques employed to assist have progressed from fertility drugs to IVF, and most recently ICSI (in which a single sperm is injected into a woman's egg in the laboratory). Sperm or egg donation are also used in cases where one or other partner is more seriously infertile, between them producing almost 1000 babies in the UK in 2008. Today IVF, including ICSI, is well established and widely available, as technology's principal 'help for the stork'. In the UK in 2007 some 47,000 cycles of IVF were carried out, resulting in 11,000 maternities, which produced nearly 14,000 babies in all (most of them of course born in 2008), including 2500 pairs of twins.

Nevertheless it is not a simple 'dial-a-baby' service, and the path to a successful pregnancy is often long and arduous for the couples involved. Although great progress has been made since the early days when success rates for IVF cycles were as low as 5 per cent, improvement beyond 23 to 24 per cent has been difficult to achieve overall. Even in the most favourable circumstances, with younger women and using their own fresh eggs, the current figure is only 32 per cent. It has been suggested that this is broadly equivalent to the natural rate, as most fertilised eggs do not in fact implant in the womb and progress into actual pregnancies, a success achieved by perhaps only one in three or four.

Even this statistic is misleading, however. Couples who are told that their IVF cycle has a one in four chance of success tend to assume that the worst case scenario is that they will need four tries to get a baby. Unfortunately this is not so. For every couple who are lucky first time there needs to be another who try seven times in order to maintain a one in four average (one cycle plus seven

175

cycles equals eight cycles, to produce two pregnancies). In practice few couples have the endurance or the finances to run to seven or more cycles, and the average is instead maintained by those who give up after two or three unsuccessful attempts.

To achieve even this success rate IVF has had to transfer more than one 'test tube' embryo into the mother's body in a single cycle. An unintended side effect of this has been a high proportion of twins, approaching 25 per cent, in the resulting pregnancies, as well as smaller numbers of triplets. The statistical basis for this, in simplified terms, is that in one in four IVF cycles one embryo successfully implants and the woman becomes pregnant. However the second embryo also has a one in four chance, and when it too succeeds twins are the result.

While some couples are happy enough, after the initial shock, to have a ready-made family at one go, thus avoiding a repeat of the IVF process, public policy is to minimise multiple births. Twin pregnancies have greater risks, twins are often born prematurely, and twins are more prone to longer-term health problems than single babies. All these factors are worse again for triplets, so that the relevant UK authority introduced new guidelines a few years ago, discouraging transfers of more than two embryos in a single cycle, other than in special cases. Current research is focused on improving the chances of pregnancy from a single embryo, and the future is likely to bring increasing restrictions on even two-embryo transfers, with a consequent fall in the proportion of twins produced by IVF.

Just to complicate things a bit further, evidence is starting to emerge that there is a higher incidence of embryo-splitting in IVF than in natural pregnancies. Once again the reasons are not fully understood, but the effect is to produce an above-average number of identical twins from IVF. Such twins stem from a single embryo, and they could occur even if the number of transfers is limited to one, so that although the proportion of twins from IVF may be reduced in the future it may still be higher than in natural pregnancies. In the shorter term two-embryo transfers continue, and with increasing availability of IVF, and public funding for couples to undertake more cycles, the number of IVF babies and of IVF twins may well continue to rise. Even triplets cannot be avoided entirely, as if two embryos successfully implant and one splits the result is three babies, two of them identical and the third non-identical.

Much less information is available about the reasons for the increase in the natural twinning rate referred to above. One possibility is that improvements in general health levels and medical care have increased the survival rate of embryos in the early weeks of pregnancy. Many die at this stage, often before the pregnancy has been confirmed or even before the woman realises that she is pregnant, while early miscarriages are frequent. Recent medical studies have found that 25 per cent of pregnancies have miscarried by the sixth week, while so-called 'clinical miscarriages' (those after the sixth week) account for a further 8 per cent. This total of 33 per cent (one in three) is a minimum, as it is unlikely that all very early pregnancies were detected, so that other estimates of 40 per cent, or even up to 60 per cent, may not be ruled out. However in an era of mainly planned pregnancies the prospective parents usually try again, so that reducing the number of miscarriages does not have a significant direct effect on the singleton birth rate. Twins are – as always – a bit different. If one of a pair of twin embryos dies in the earliest stages of pregnancy while the other survives, the miscarriage may well not be noticed, and the result is a single baby. Improvements in embryo survival may have reduced the number of such cases, resulting in an increase in the number of twins.

This, it must be admitted, is mainly speculation, but more definite reasons are hard to come by. Advances in medical care have reduced the death rate of babies before, during and immediately after birth, and as twins are more vulnerable they may have benefited disproportionately, perhaps contributing to an increase in the twinning rate. The effect can only have been small, however, as neonatal and perinatal death rates have been low for many years in developed countries. It has also been suggested that as older women are more likely to have twins the trend towards starting families later may have contributed to the higher twinning rate, but again the effect can only have been limited. The increase in average age at childbirth has only been slow and small in recent years, and the growth of IVF has influenced this, as most IVF mothers are significantly older. None of these ideas seem to provide a full explanation, so that for the moment the effect is more apparent than the causes.

But what *is* a twin?

To most people the answer seems obvious, but in fact there are many variations. The usual technical definition of twins used to be two babies born at the same time from one woman and resulting from a single menstrual cycle. IVF has made this obsolete, as if more embryos than are needed for one cycle are successfully produced the remainder are usually frozen for use on a later occasion, either in case the woman then has insufficient eggs or to avoid the heavy dose of hormone drugs needed to release them. Hence babies arising from the same menstrual cycle may be born a couple of years apart, and where un-needed embryos are donated to help the seriously infertile they may even be born to different women. No one would regard the resulting children as twins, but even among those more readily accepted as such there were differences even before technology intervened.

Fraternal twins are the usual type, arising from two eggs fertilised by two separate sperms, whether naturally or by IVF. In the womb these babies sit in separate sacs, each with its own placenta, and they are much the same as other babies, apart from sharing their first nine months in an increasingly tight space. They are no more alike than ordinary brothers and sisters, with on average 50 per cent of their distinctive genetic make-up in common. Nevertheless there are some special cases which also challenge the simple definition.

Half-twins arise when naturally conceived twins have different fathers, in a process known as superfecundation. Eggs remain viable inside a woman for at least one day and sperm can survive for up to five days, so that if more than one egg has been released in a cycle it is possible for two men to get a look in! In a case in Dallas, Texas, a woman and her partner noticed that their eleven-month-old twins Justin and Jordan had quite different facial features, and a DNA test revealed that they were in fact only half-brothers. The shocked mother then confessed to having had an affair around the time of their conception. How common such 'twins' are can only be speculation, as no doubt some women would feel 'Mum's the word' to be the best motto in the circumstances.

Twins of slightly different ages can result from another rare process, superfoetation. When an embryo implants in the womb this suppresses further ovulation, but occasionally the mother can release an egg in a new menstrual cycle. With normal sexual activity continuing this too can be fertilised, and in some cases the embryo may also implant. This leads to a twin pregnancy, although the 'twins' might be several weeks different in age. When Amelia went for her twelve-week scan, little Ame was too small to be measured although her sister Lia was the expected size for that stage, and the doctors suggested that they might have been conceived up to three weeks apart. After an emergency Caesarean Lia was born at week 32 weighing 3.0 kg (6 lb 11 oz), while Ame tipped the scales at only 2.2 kg (4 lb 13 oz), suggesting that she was in week 29. Happily both girls made good progress.

Twins of different ages, or at least with quite different birthdays, can also result from complications in the birth process. Sandra gave birth to her daughter Chloe in Edinburgh on 11 June 2000, 28 days after having had brother Edward very prematurely on 14 May. He weighed just 0.8 kg (1 lb 12 oz). Chloe, weighing 1.2 kg (2 lb 11 oz), was delivered by Caesarean after fears that an infection might develop from Edward's placenta, which had remained in the womb. The largest recorded gap between twins was in the US, where Peggy's first twin Hanna was born on 11 November 1995, followed 83 days later by Eric on 2 February 1996. Another case with a 38-day gap, spreading over from 1987 into 1988, was reported in Italy.

Twins from separate wombs can also arise, as some woman do in fact have two of these vital organs, a condition not as rare as it might seem, because in many cases it is not noticed unless circumstances dictate. It may be possible to become pregnant in either or both, and although the chances of doing so at the same time are small it does happen, a condition also know as superfoetation. Moreover it might occur in separate menstrual cycles, giving twins of slightly different ages too. Sarah from Michigan needed two Caesarean sections, one for each womb, to deliver her daughters Kaylin and Valerie seven weeks before time, and as she already had a ten-month-old son she had her hands full!

Identical twins are less common than normal fraternal twins, although much more frequent than the unusual types of fraternal twins mentioned above. Their origin is different, starting from just one fertilised egg, which may divide at any time from the earliest stage to up to sixteen days later. In about a third of cases this occurs in the first five days, while the egg is still in the fallopian tube and before it reaches the womb. As a result these early-

179

splitters implant separately, like fraternal twins, and develop with their own placentas, amnion (inner sac) and chorion (outer sac). The remaining two-thirds implant jointly and have a single placenta and chorion, but each has its own amniotic sac, although in rare cases they may have to share that too.

Conjoined twins may result when the fertilised egg splits late, after thirteen days, and their fused bodies may share essential organs. They are always identical but are very rare, and doctors suspect that most cases abort naturally before being diagnosed. Some 40 to 60 per cent are stillborn, and most of the remainder die soon after birth, but even the few who survive this stage have only a small chance for the longer term. Viability depends on the degree of sharing, and although surgical techniques have improved in recent years, allowing some twins to be separated, the operations are still risky. Even when successful it is unusual for both twins to survive, as a number of highly publicised cases confirm.

Parents are thus faced with agonising decisions, as the chance of life for one twin might involve sacrificing the other, probably the weaker. Even that much success is uncertain. Twins Faith and Hope, joined from the breastbone to the navel, underwent separation surgery in London but both died, the one 23 days after the other. The parents of Mary and Jodie, fused together at the spine, did not want to take the risk, but in the year 2000 a British court ordered an attempt at separation. Mary died, but her sister survived.

In earlier times such twins were regarded as freaks, and one pair, Chang and Eng Bunker, found fame touring the United States during the nineteenth century, including a brief stint with a travelling circus. They were born in 1811 in Siam (Thailand), and they were the original 'Siamese twins', a term which is now outmoded but still appears in the newspapers. The men were joined by a strip of cartilage from the chest, and although their livers were fused they were complete, so that they could have been surgically separated today. Despite this handicap they lived to the age of 63, and they seem to have had an adventurous sex life, as they reputedly fathered over twenty children. When Chang died after a serious illness, his brother, who had been healthy until then, passed away just a couple of hours later.

Halfway-house twins? There is speculation that there may be an intermediate type of twins, genetically more similar to each other than fraternals but less alike than identicals. This unconfirmed theory suggests that the mother's egg itself may split, and that both parts may then be separately fertilised. Every egg and every sperm are slightly different genetically, which is why ordinary siblings are not identical, but such halfway-house twins would be identical in respect of the portion of their genetic material derived from their mother's single egg. On the other hand fertilisation by two separate sperms from their father would give rise to differences in the remainder. Whether such twins actually exist is still an open question.

Triplets are much rarer than twins, but they still come in several variants, as they can originate from three, two or even only one egg. Three eggs produce fully fraternal triplets, but if there are only two fertilised eggs and one splits the result is two identical and one non-identical members of the threesome. Very occasionally a single fertilised egg may split more than once, giving rise to three identical babies. Some of the unusual possibilities mentioned above for twins also exist for triplets, but as triplets are themselves infrequent the likelihood in practice is negligible.

Triplets only occurred naturally in one in 8500 pregnancies in the UK in 1977, although even this may have been increased by infertility drug treatment, as the underlying natural figure used to be viewed as one in 10,000. In 1977 there were 76 higher-order multiple births, all triplets apart from a few sets of quads. Multiple IVF embryo transfers initially produced a sharp increase in this number, to 290 in the year 2000, but restrictions then introduced brought this down to 143 by 2003. Numbers have since increased with the total birth-rate, to 190 in 2008, of which 33 were the result of IVF treatment. Nevertheless the naturally conceived number was one per 5000 maternities, so that, as with twins, there has also been a significant increase in the natural triplet rate in recent years.

Identical triplets are yet rarer, so rare that there are no meaningful statistics. Estimates vary from one in 100 million down to one in 160,000 pregnancies. This is little more than guesswork, but the membership of Germany's ABC Club may provide some indication, even if lacking a statistical basis. This club is only open to triplets and higher-order multiples, and of its 2503 sets of triplets 46 are reported to be identical. Taking the past general triplet rate as one in 10,000 as noted above, this would imply a natural identical triplet rate of one in about half a million maternities, or something like one set a year in Britain.

Higher-order multiples also occur, but with diminishing frequency as numbers rise. Germany's ABC Club has 125 sets of quads, 12 sets of quins, and 3 sets of sextuplets, but none of them are fully identical. Risks rise with the multiple, so that survival becomes as significant as conception in determining the actual number of such births. Less obviously, any baby, whether a singleton, twin or triplet, may have started life as part of a larger unit, in which one or more sibling embryos failed to survive the early stages of pregnancy. More of us may be twins than we realise!

'I paint objects as I think them, not as I see them'
(*Picasso*)

Consciously or sub-consciously, most people associate the term 'identical' with twins, and as a result many focus on the similarities they can identify and tend to overlook the differences. Parents, who perceive their own children as clearly different from each other, are often startled by this. One mother scathingly recalls being asked by another, after a year of meeting on the nursery school run, whether her twin boys, one with wavy brown locks and the other with straight blond hair, were identical. Another was even more surprised to be asked the same question about her boy and girl twins! Shared home experience, common behavioural traits, even dressing twins in the same clothes, can foster the identical image, even when they are not. Many parents do not themselves know for certain whether their twins are 'identical', the actual meaning of which is discussed in the next chapter.

The only way to be quite sure is to carry out a DNA test, but as there is usually no medical reason for this it is not done routinely at maternity units. Noting that there appears to have been a single placenta can make it highly likely that twins are identical, while viewing a single outer sac on a scan also indicates a strong probability. However, as this is not the purpose of making such observations, they are not necessarily reliable as indicators, and in any case there may still be exceptions. For 'early splitter' identical twins who implant separately in the womb, and have two placentas and outer sacs, there are no such pointers, and curious parents can only guess unless they are prepared to arrange DNA tests privately. Perhaps the only certainty is that twins of opposite sexes cannot be identical.

As a result there are no valid statistics, but medical research suggests that the naturally occurring incidence of identical twins is much the same throughout the world, irrespective of ethnic background. The rate is variously quoted as 3 or 4 pairs per 1000 maternities, with some sources compromising at 3.5. This suggests that it is not linked to heredity and that such twins occur more or less at random, so that the well-known tendency for twins to run in families is assumed to relate only to fraternal twins. The frequency of the latter is also linked to ethnicity, so that for example twins are very common in Nigeria and quite unusual in Japan. Hence while the commonly quoted figure that around one-third of all twins are identical may be a valid estimate for the world as a whole, the proportion varies from place to place. For Britain a lower figure of perhaps a quarter seems appropriate, and given the limited amount of actual data available a large margin of error has to be applied even to that.

Some parents live with uncertainty, while others develop false certainties. Opera singer Sinéad's twins Isabelle and Emilie are four, and scans during pregnancy showed that they were in individual sacs and had separate placentas. The doctors confirmed the latter point at the time of the delivery, explaining that the twins were thus much more likely to be fraternal than identical. The parents are not convinced, as the girls look very similar, with the same hair and eye colouring and shared physical attributes, so that friends and even some family members have difficulty in telling them apart. The same applies to Tracey's eleven-year-old daughters, both willowy, with the same dark hair, eyes and skin. However she had always believed that they could not be identical as they were in separate sacs in the womb. Learning that this does not in fact exclude identical twins came as something of a shock to her.

For some parents, and for some twins themselves, knowing whether they are identical can seem important. Others are simply happy to take things as they experience them. In practical terms it rarely matters unless medical issues arise, as if certain hereditary conditions are developed by the one there is a considerable risk that the other may also be affected, which is much less the case with fraternals. At a more prosaic level, parents of twins might want to know before contemplating another pregnancy, as the risk of having a second set would be much greater if the first pair were fraternal. This particular kind of lightning strikes twice surprisingly frequently!

Heredity can also play strange tricks. At the other extreme to parents who wonder whether their twins are identical, a British couple have two very clearly different sets. The father is of West Indian origin while the mother is Caucasian, and in their first set of twins, born in Hampshire in 2001, the blue-eyed, red-haired girl takes after her mother, whereas her sister has black skin and hair like her father. With the second set, born in 2008, once again one of the girls is dark-skinned, and the other is white.

Bounty bar!

Even Buckingham Palace has taken note of the upward trend in multiple births. Queen Victoria initiated the Sovereign's Bounty, providing poorer parents of newborn triplets with a payment from the privy purse in recognition of the extra expenses they would incur. The gift of £3 for triplets (and £4 for quads) was made 'when the children all survive, the parents being respectable but too poor to meet the unforeseen demands for providing for them at once'. After 1938 this proviso was abolished, and the bounty was paid to all families having a higher-order multiple birth, with no strings attached.

By December 1957 needy families were supported, at least in theory, by the welfare state, and the bounty's value had dwindled so much that the payment was replaced by a congratulatory message from the Queen to the proud parents. As triplet births continued to rise following the success of infertility treatments, the monarchy finally stopped sending out even the messages. The official explanation: 'In February 1995, owing to the increased frequency of multiple births due to medical advances, it was decided that messages of congratulation would no longer be sent.'

One face, one voice, one habit ... and two persons

(Shakespeare, *Twelfth Night*)

Identical twins. Or are they?

Identical twins, indistinguishable alter egos who no one can tell apart, are long-established stereotypes. Shakespeare's play *The Comedy of Errors* involves two pairs, respectively gentlemen and their servants. And yet, as the present author met pair after pair, doubts started to creep in. One twin was left-handed, the other not. Others had hair which fell naturally in different ways. Two young men had heads of rather different shapes, the only way, they said, that anyone other than their closest intimates could be sure which they were talking to. In most cases, it appears, fingerprints show significant variations. So how identical is identical?

Until the latter part of the twentieth century science had no answer. The mechanism of embryo-splitting was well known, and hence such twins were expected to be identical. Some differences could be put down to developmental influences, learned behaviour or individual taste. But fingerprints? Evidently there were some questions for which the answers had yet to be found. The solution, or at least the key to further progress, lay in the identification first of DNA and then of the human genome, arguably the greatest scientific advances of the era. To the layman, however, these subjects remain as mystifying as quantum mechanics or the Big Bang theory, and we need some guidance through the labyrinth.

The double helix. Where it all begins

The double helix, two intertwined spirals which form the molecular structure of deoxyribonucleic acid, DNA for short, carries the base data comprising the genetic make-up of all living things. This is packaged into chromosomes, which in turn carry the genes which determine what and who we are. So far so good, but as yet scientists have not analysed the function of 97 per cent of human DNA, sometimes referred to as 'junk DNA' precisely because it seems to have no function. One expert rejects the term, 'as this implies that it is not useful, whereas we simply don't know what much of it does.' Apparently what it does *not* do is to carry codes for the key proteins which shape our existence, the function of the other vital 3 per cent, but that is almost as much as can so far be said. As so often in science, it seems that the more we know the more we find that we have to learn.

To pass on the whole DNA structure from generation to generation, both the egg and the sperm carry an amazing three billion encoded letters on their 23 chromosomes, which fuse at conception to form the full human complement of 46. The individual variations arise because every egg and every sperm are slightly different, even when produced by the same woman or man, which is why siblings and even fraternal twins are not identical. Hence every newly conceived embryo is unique, carrying within it the specific DNA which determines the characteristics of the prospective baby as a human individual. Nevertheless the similarities are vastly greater than the differences. Astonishingly, it appears that all humans share 99.9 per cent of the same DNA, despite widely different ethnic backgrounds and individual physical and mental characteristics.

Spitting images. Or splitting images?

Identical twins arise when, at some time within the first sixteen days, a fertilised egg spontaneously splits. At that point both halves share the same original DNA, but the tiny twins are likely to remain truly identical for only a relatively short time. The DNA molecule is not a totally fixed structure, and as human cells and the DNA within them are constantly renewed in the course of growth and life, this provides the opportunity for mutations to occur. In the context of the whole molecule these are very minor, but they can nevertheless be sufficient to cause small changes in the genetic code, and hence in the characteristics of individual people.

Mutations are possible throughout life, and they are cumulative in their effect, so that the older a pair of identical twins the more genetic variations there are likely to be. Changes in one of the embryos during the earliest stages after splitting could in principle affect some factor which might produce visible differences in the eventual twins, such as eye colour, but as the main physical features are fixed quite early in development this is not a common occurrence. In fact most mutations produce no detectable

187

variations, and those which do are likely to be barely noticeable, which is why 'identical' twins still appear identical even though at the fundamental level they are not.

This fact is recognised in the scientific world, where the term 'identical' is not used. Instead such twins are described as 'monozygotic', a zygote being a fertilised egg. The logical Germans do likewise, referring to 'one-egg twins' or 'two-egg twins', which if rather literal is at least less confusing. However English being what it is, 'identical' will continue to be used in the rest of this chapter.

One variation which may occur in the earliest stages gives rise to so-called 'mirror twins'. This is thought to apply to perhaps 25 per cent of identical twins, in cases where the fertilised egg splits quite late, at around nine to twelve days after conception. Some of the characteristics of such twins may be the same but arranged in opposite patterns, so that one may be left-handed and the other right-handed, or their hair may naturally fall on opposite sides.

Other variations develop progressively during life, in a process known as 'epigenetic drift'. Scientists have established that the genes of very young identical twins are normally effectively the same, but that differences become more readily identifiable as they age. This may or may not produce recognisable although minor differences. Oddly, however, research also suggests that certain traits, such as scores on IQ tests or other personality factors, may actually become more alike as identical twins get older. Once more there are as yet no clear explanations.

DNA plus ...... ?

There is more to it than just DNA. Proteins from the parents are present in the egg and the sperm, and these become attached to the DNA in the embryo in a process known as genomic imprinting. This determines how the DNA from the parents will manifest itself in the resulting baby. Should these proteins alter after the egg has split, this could lead to changes creating differences between identical twins. In one unusually evident case doctors observed a severe growth setback in one twin in the womb, although her sister's growth was as expected. After birth her head was also found to be misshapen whereas her sister's was normal, but a DNA test showed that despite their very different appearances the twins were nevertheless identical.

Subtle differences may also arise due to conditions in the womb, where even identical twins have varying experiences, depending on factors such as which is lying where at particular times. Some characteristics, known as phenotypes, are governed by a combination of genetic determination and developmental environment. This can start in the womb and may affect aspects of physical appearance. Fingerprint patterns are an example. Although genes provide the basis, physical contact during early development also has an influence. During this stage the one foetus's fingers will come into contact with different surfaces and in different ways to the other twin's, so that their eventual fingerprints may differ.

More obvious physical factors can also play a part. All twins experience unusually cramped conditions in the womb if the pregnancy runs to, or near to, full term, and this may have visible effects on features such as head shape. Like all babies, identical twins may be affected by mischance or accident while in the womb or during the birth, but not necessarily in the same way or to the same extent. For example the shape of a baby's head is sometimes affected by problems during the delivery, but twins, whether identical or fraternal, may have quite different experiences, in extreme cases one being born naturally and the other by Caesarean. One possible problem specific to identical twins is twin-to-twin transfusion, a potentially fatal condition in which one baby's blood is drained into the other's body through the blood vessels in the shared placenta. Twins surviving this trauma often have widely differing birth weights, and the smaller may never catch up in later life.

Experience is a great teacher ....

But does it result in differing characteristics between identical twins? Physical environment can obviously produce superficial variations, so that one twin who has spent years working out of doors in a hot country will probably look older than the other who has had an office job in Britain. Differences in diet, exercise, or consumption of tobacco, alcohol or other drugs can also have a visible effect. More significant, however, is the long-running 'nature' or 'nurture' debate about influences on character traits for people in general. Twins, particularly identical ones, are a potential source of information on this subject, and serious research studies go back at least as far as 1875. 'Nature', that is the inherent individual characteristics with which a person is born, is much better understood since the development of the science of genetics, although this is much more true for physical features than for character, personality or psychological traits. 'Nurture', the upbringing and environment to which a person is exposed from birth onwards, has always been controversial, as causes and effects are difficult to isolate and evaluate, while contradictory examples abound, whatever theory is put forward.

Identical twins, presumed to share a common 'nature' through near-identical DNA, seem to offer a control through which the varying effects of 'nurture' can be studied. Perversely, though, twins tend to share a much more similar upbringing and environment even than normal siblings. Where one child is older than another, the younger will be brought up by more experienced parents, while externally the family circumstances may have changed. Perhaps Dad has been promoted and there is more money about. Perhaps Mum has gone back to work after the birth of the last planned child, or vice versa, perhaps she has to stay at home as child-minding cannot be afforded for two youngsters. The age-old argument between siblings as to whether the eldest or the youngest had it hardest makes the point.

Hence situations in which identical twins have been brought up separately have been seized upon eagerly as the basis for more valid studies. Some striking similarities have been found, suggesting that genetic factors do indeed have a significant role in shaping an individual's personality, but even here some caveats are needed. Such cases are rare, so that the size of the studies has necessarily been small. Moreover by definition they involve unusual family circumstances, which resulted in the twins being separated, and probably one or both being adopted. The actual quality of the studies is hard for the non-expert to assess, but it is well known that in many fields, particularly non-quantifiable ones, researchers tend to find what they are looking for.

That said, let us consider the 'Jim twins', the subjects of a Minnesota University study in 1979. Identical twins Jim Lewis and Jim Springer were separated as small babies, raised in different adoptive families, and had no contact with each other until they were 39. Both learned as children that they had had a twin, but

Springer and his family believed that the other had died. Eventually Lewis decided to investigate, and after a long search through court records he finally tracked his brother down.

He reportedly described their first meeting as 'like looking in a mirror', and the parallels did not stop there. Not so surprisingly, the brothers were the same height and weight, and they had similar facial expressions, IQs and handwriting. More remarkably, they had also both married twice, first to a Linda and then to a Betty, they each had a son with virtually the same names, James Alan and James Allen, both had dogs called Toy, they drank the same beer and smoked the same cigarettes, drove the same make of car, and took holidays on the same small beach in Florida. Or so it was said.

Amazing genetic effects, or mere – if startling – coincidences? A Chevrolet was one of the most common American cars of the period, and the names Linda, Betty and Alan (however spelled) are not unusual, while James of course derives from the sons being named after the fathers. Curiously, but without genetic influence, it appears that both of the twins had been called the same name by their adoptive parents. Nor are astonishing coincidences that rare, as readers of 'true life stories' in the popular press soon realise. During a discussion with the author of this book, one of the contributors noted that both were wearing identical but unusual Swiss watches, a point which researchers might well have considered significant had there been any genetic link. By themselves the Jim twins prove little, and comparable studies are few. The 'nature' or 'nurture' debate doubtless has plenty of life in it yet.

Twins studies. A medical perspective

Studies based on twins play a much more significant role in the medical world. Trials of new medications or procedures on identical twins provide unique opportunities to compare the outcomes on effectively the same genetic person, treated and untreated. The medical histories of twins can also help to unlock the secrets of specific diseases. Olivia developed a potentially fatal form of leukaemia at the age of two, whereas her identical sister Isabella did not, although both were born with the same genetic defect making them equally susceptible. Doctors then discovered that Olivia had subsequently had a genetic mutation, which may have been caused by a common cold or other relatively harmless virus, increasing her risk. During the progress of the disease the doctors were able to monitor both the sick twin and her healthy sister, thus giving them a special insight into its early stages. As a result new procedures were developed which allow less intensive chemotherapy to be given in some cases, reducing side-effects and making the process more bearable for patient and family.

Life in duplicate

Given that monozygotic ('one-egg') twins are very nearly genetically identical, close physical resemblances and matching abilities are logical consequences. So too are shared susceptibility or resistance to particular diseases, and similar degrees of proneness to conditions such as obesity or baldness. Although rare in practice, transplants of organs or skin grafts are much easier between identical twins, as near-perfect matches ensure that rejection is much less likely than in other cases, even between normal siblings. Measures of intelligence such as IQ tests also usually produce very similar results. Psychology and character are much harder to evaluate, leaving open the question which underlies the 'nature' or 'nurture' debate. How closely do similarities in personality correspond to the evident physical duplication in identical twins?

Answers are harder to come by. Anecdotal evidence is almost always concerned with remarkable parallels, while not only outside observers but even family members tend to focus on similarities and overlook or discount differences. A further complication is the tendency of identical twins themselves to stress their closeness, at least among those pairs who 'go public' by joining twins clubs or by being prepared to take part in studies or interviews. There may indeed be others who are, feel, or wish to be more different, but probably for this very reason are less in evidence.

Stories abound. After a long flight home twin girls teased or threatened their father that they would reveal to the immigration officer at London Heathrow that their passports had the wrong photos in them. In the Chinese city of Yiwu customers were astounded by the dedication of a couple who ran a restaurant, opening it up at 6 a.m. and staying until closing time at 3 a.m. the following morning. What they didn't realise was that the proprietors were two pairs of identical twins married to each other. Identical twin lads surprised their driving examiner by achieving exactly the same score in their tests, which they passed despite both stalling at the same set of traffic lights. Two Polish men, identical twins, capped parallel school performances by gaining admission to study the same subject at the same Oxford college. But even they have been upstaged by the identical triplet women who performed a similar feat at Cambridge University.

Underlying such anecdotes is the tendency for identical twins to be viewed as a unit rather than as individuals, a tendency which is bound to be reflected in twins' views of themselves. Amusing though the story may be, the fact is that a father confused his own daughters' passport photographs. The customers in Yiwu reportedly called the restaurant twins 'the robots', inadvertently giving expression to the depersonalisation inherent in their inability not so much to tell them apart as even to realise that they *were* different people. The stories about the Oxford and Cambridge entrants are recounted not because of the gratifying achievements of the individuals, but only because they were performed in duplicate or triplicate.

The Yiwu marriage of two sets of identical twins may not be the remarkable coincidence which it at first appears. Two identical young men interviewed during the research for this book were actively seeking a suitable pair of twin women with romance in mind. No one else, they seemed to feel, could fully understand the complex nature of being an identical twin. 'My other half' is a standard phrase in marital relationships, but identical twins also have another, more literal, 'other half'.

Relativity and genetics

The complicated relationship between identical twins does not stop with them, but passes on to the next generation. The Sanders family in Texas also has two pairs of identical twins married to each other, and the couples have five children between them. As both mothers are genetically almost identical, as are both fathers, it follows that all the children, from whichever couple, have genetic make-ups equivalent to full brothers and sisters. Just to complicate matters further, two of the children are themselves identical twins. Even in the more common situation in which identical twins find quite separate partners, their respective children have the genetic relationship of half-brothers or half-sisters rather than cousins. Nevertheless all the relevant children from marriages of whichever kind involving identical twins are technically first cousins, and hence able to marry each other in most countries. However their genetic links are equivalent to half-siblings or full siblings, and such marriages are almost everywhere prohibited because of the age-old incest taboo.

DNA again. A testing question

DNA tests are well known from crime reports in the newspapers and detective films on television, although they have only been used in criminal courts in Britain since the mid-1980s. They have achieved some spectacular successes in providing evidence and convicting offenders who had in some cases evaded justice for years. More sombrely, they have also exposed a number of past injustices. One innocent man had served 27 years of a life sentence before DNA tests on samples from the scene of the crime were found not to match his own. His conviction was quashed, but no one could give him back 27 years of his life.

A DNA test also established that two 28-year-old Spanish women brought up separately since birth were in fact identical twins. One had been swapped with a third baby in a hospital mix-up, which only came to light in 2001. One of the twins walked into a shop, but did not respond to the greeting of an assistant who was a close friend of her sister. Questions followed, and gradually two and two were put together. All three women were eventually awarded substantial compensation.

As identical twins have DNA which is not in fact completely identical, as described above, then we might expect DNA tests to be able to distinguish between them. In fact this is hardly ever the case. The reason is that so-called DNA matching is nothing of the kind. Even though only something like 0.1 per cent (a one-thousandth part) of human DNA carries all the codes which separate one individual from another, a very large number of comparisons would have to be made to truly match two samples. Instead analysts concentrate on specific parts of the genome called microsatellite markers, which consist of short repeated sequences. These markers and sequences are mainly inherited from the parents, but with minor mutations which make each person unique. Hence experts review the pattern of repeats for various standard markers to see if there is a match, at least to this extent, between two DNA samples. This is sensitive enough to ensure that if there is such a match the samples come from the same person, and if there is not that they come from two different people.

Except in the case of identical twins. The DNA molecule is so large and complex that the number of places where minor variations could arise due to differing mutations between identical twins is enormous. The chances of them occurring on one of the markers used in tests are minute, so that the standard test cannot distinguish between such twins. Theoretically more and more markers could be examined until a difference *was* found, but this is not a practical proposition, so far at least. Away from the criminal world, commercial DNA testing is available to determine whether twins are identical or fraternal, known as zygosity tests, and these may use as few as twelve of these satellite markers to achieve this level of differentiation.

Who dunnit?

The 'DNA test loophole' for identical twins gives rise to some unusual problems. Paternity tests, for example, are also based on DNA, and hence they too are unable to distinguish between identical twins. In a case in Montreal a man sought to establish paternity rights over 'his' little boy after the breakdown of a relationship, but the mother admitted that she had also been sleeping with his identical twin brother at the relevant time. As DNA tests did not help, the judge was forced to conclude that 'it is impossible to determine who the father is'. In a similar case in Missouri a man denied paternity, claiming that his identical twin brother was the real father. Again DNA tests could not resolve the issue, and in this case the judge chose instead to accept the mother's testimony.

A number of cases in the criminal world come into the 'stranger than fiction' category. Thus one or other of a pair of Malaysian identical twins escaped conviction and hanging because of uncertainty as to which of them had been trafficking opium.

One was caught red-handed, but his brother arrived on the scene immediately afterwards, and the police became confused as to which they had actually arrested. DNA tests got them no further, and the judge was forced to throw the case out for lack of evidence of identity, commenting that 'I can't be sending the wrong man to the gallows'.

DNA was also at the centre of a case in Berlin. There, in a scene reminiscent of a well-known film, security cameras recorded masked men lowering themselves into the hall of the city's leading department store, before escaping with valuable jewellery. A glove was discovered at the scene of the crime, and a bead of dried sweat was sufficient for a DNA test. The police thought that they were in luck when their computer records provided a match – except that it provided two matches. The suspects thus identified were identical twins, but although one of them was clearly guilty the absence of other evidence meant that neither of them could be convicted. Nor has the jewellery been recovered!

The perfect gift

for a twin, the parents or grandparents of twins, or those expecting twins

A copy of this book!

Enquiries and orders by e-mail to

thetwinsbook@aol.co.uk